FOR JACK

All proceeds from the sale of this book, after printing costs,
will go to the Diocese of Kildare & Leighlin.

MY LIFE IN
YOUR HANDS

THOUGHTS & WORDS OF
FR. JOHN CUMMINS

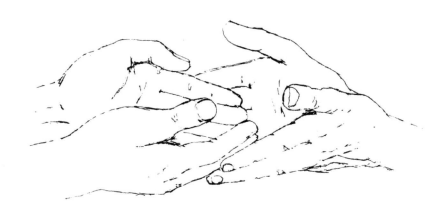

LITURGICAL YEAR A

TABLE OF CONTENTS

FAMILY ACKNOWLEDGEMENT

When we think of John, we remember many things. To his family he was a much-loved son, brother, nephew, uncle and brother-in-law. He had an easy manner, a keen intellect, an energetic spirit and a unique sense of humour. He was a scamp!

To his friends he was a loyal, trusted confidant, and the source of much mirth and mischief.

To the people he served, he was their priest...and a priest was all and everything he ever wanted to be.

He enjoyed making connections and dedicated his life to connecting people with God.

Following John's death, parishioners and friends spoke fondly of his homilies and how they provoked thought and provided solace.

John saved his sermons, initially in physical files, and latterly electronically. We feel that it is appropriate to continue John's work by publishing his words. These writings were created to be heard rather than read. We can hear John's voice when we read these words.

This book would not be possible without David Connaughton whose IT knowledge allowed access to John's files. We are very grateful to Dominic and Neasa Reigh who facilitated this.

We wholeheartedly thank Paddy Pender, Julie Kavanagh, Fr. Gerard Ahern, Maeve Mahon and Joe O'Brien for their tireless work in curating this book with us.

Bishop Denis Nulty provided approval and wise advice at the beginning of this project. We thank him for his introduction and kind friendship over the last few years. Bishop Ger Nash, John's fellow adventurer and friend, has provided a beautiful foreword. We are very grateful to him for this and so many other kind deeds since he and John were students.

We have received wonderful support from John's brother priests in the diocese of Kildare and Leighlin. They have our deep gratitude.

In the aftermath of John's death we were overwhelmed by the kindness and generosity of the people of Abbeyleix, Ballyroan, Carlow, Naas, Newbridge and John's many friends. We will be forever grateful to you all.

The words, "Father I place my life in your hands", which featured on John's ordination card were central to his relationship with God and the nature of vocational life, inspired the title of this book

The illustration on the front cover was also a feature of John's ordination card. This was drawn by Neasa Hogan from a photograph of John's hands with those of his father.

We hope this book provides food for thought and companionship on the reader's faith journey.

- The Cummins Family

It is a great privilege to write these few words as a foreword to the collection of reflections for the Sundays of Liturgical Year A. Especially as these are the collected words of John Cummins who as fellow student, friend and holiday companion for nearly thirty years inspired and challenged me with his wisdom, his wit and his insights into human life and the priesthood we were both privileged to be called to.

We began our journey in September 1984 in First Year in Maynooth and over the seven years, friendship grew and strengthened. We were ordained in 1991 and despite many different ministries and sometimes different countries, we kept in contact and the annual holiday was always carefully planned early each year so that the time would be kept free.

The tragedy of his untimely death has left a void in all our lives, especially at those times when John would have been part of our circle. For his family, it is Christmas, Birthdays and Anniversaries. For us, his friends, it is the holiday or the Maynooth reunion or his spring dinner for those who are part of our circle in Maynooth. We came together over three days in Spring 2019 to deal with the crushing news and to be a presence to his family who were so special to him and who in turn, loved him greatly.

And then like Peter, went back fishing, - because we had to, because life doesn't stand still, but also to bury our grief in the bits and pieces of everyday. But like Peter on the lakeshore, the Resurrection is a reality for us. We are people of faith, shaky maybe at times, but nevertheless believing that our human lives are simply chapters in a great and longer story. Our eternal relationship with God.

John was a man who believed this and lived out his belief. Like St Paul we could call many witnesses to this, but I will name just one. John's solid and constant prayer life built on his understanding of his relationship with Christ, first as a man and then as a priest. His sense of priesthood was clear – it was the defining relationship of his life, but because he understood it so well, it meant that every other relationship whether with family, parish, colleagues, diocese or friends had the mark of Christ about it. He loved the idea of the priest as the "Interpreter of Life", helping people to make sense of their lives and to see the presence of God in its complexity.

As you use this book, as a person of prayer, as a leader of Liturgy, as a preacher, may the goodness that was in Johns' life and words seep into your soul and may you find the journey of life lit up with his nourishing words. May it take the tangled conversations of life and interpret them so that the presence of God shines through.

- Ger Nash
Bishop of Ferns

INTRODUCTION

I remember the evening well. It was a Wednesday. There was a hard frost the night before. It's a phone call I will never forget. I think every tractor and truck was out that evening on the road as I made the broken-hearted journey from Carlow to Abbeyleix. John had died too soon, I knew it then and know it now. Taken away from us in the prime of his life.

The days that followed were in a sense a triduum of tears that flowed from the Cathedral of the Assumption in Carlow - where he was Administrator for eleven years, to the Church of the Holy Rosary, Abbeyleix - where he was Parish Priest for too brief a time, to St. Conleth's in Newbridge - a church associated with so many sacramental moments in the life of John and the Cummins' family. The days and weeks that followed brought post bags with cards and letters from people who were impacted in so many ways by John's too short life.

On occasions I take up those cards and letters and read them again. In ways the reading of them brings into focus the presence of the one we have loved in life but lost to death. And now with this publication of 'My Life in Your Hands' we have John's own words in homilies preached in many settings from Cathedrals to Basilicas, from Churches to colleges, from schools to homes.

Maybe it was a feastday; perhaps it was a funeral; often it was a Sunday – John was always prepared. And because he was so prepared, he has left behind a treasure trove of homilies preached. We are indebted to the small editorial team of family and friends who had the unenviable task of choosing what to include. The title 'My Life in Your Hands' is taken from the quotation of Luke 23:46 on John's Mortuary Card. The quotation is rounded off on the same card with the phrase "it is your face O Lord that I seek" (Ps. 26). When John preached he gave us, each time, a glimpse of the face of God.

I love the Irish phrase: "Ní imithe uainn atá, ach imithe romhainn" - they are not gone from us, but gone before us. John loved Irish, in fact he loved languages, as anyone who ever travelled on pilgrimage with him will attest. And at heart John Cummins was, we all know, a wonderful wordsmith. This compilation, the first of three, corresponding with the liturgical cycle, offers the reader the words John preached in Abbeyleix, Carlow and Naas. May John, who now looks on the face of God, help all of us to see God's face through a selection of his homilies, over his twenty-eight years of priesthood.

- Denis Nulty
Bishop of Kildare & Leighlin

ALWAYS HAVE A REASON FOR THE HOPE
THAT IS WITHIN YOU.

(1 PET 3:15)

Always have a reason for the hope that is within you. (1Pet 3:15)

In reflecting on how I came to be a priest and still remain one, I'm surprised at how little has changed. While experience has tempered my idealism and some new factors, events and people have entered into the story, either challenging or sustaining me, much of what originally inspired me holds true. I'm very optimistic about priesthood. I like being a priest; I believe in the priesthood. In answering the call to priesthood, I believe that I am fulfilling God's plan for me, and as such, it is the most authentic way of life that I could possibly choose. But yet I wonder if that would be enough to keep someone else going; at the end of the day, it's a personal story, unique to every priest. St. Peter reminds us always to have a reason for the hope that is within you; in other words, know what it is that keeps you going. This essay offers me the opportunity to reflect on what keeps me going, on the reasons for the hope that is within me, that deep confidence in the love of God which never departs.

I was ordained on June 16, 1991, a day on which Kildare lost the National League Final Replay to Dublin.* My first four years of ministry were spent in Naas where I learnt a huge amount and where my enthusiasm and idealism both grew and matured. 1995 took me to Rome and further studies. Life in the Eternal City was a joy, although I'm afraid I didn't develop anything like the inside track on the Vatican that many at home thought was a given. In fact, I had little interest in life across the Tiber; it was part of the broader picture, a privilege to be a spectator, but that was enough. Being in Rome opened my eyes to the limitations of our perspective in Ireland, both as Church and as society. But it also opened up a truly global city, a city with its finger on the pulse of the world. For the ancient Romans, Rome was the centre of civilisation; I didn't think that that had changed much. Back from Rome, I spent 5 years as chaplain in the Institute of Technology, Carlow. Here I encountered the semi-state structure and had the opportunity to compare that institution with Church, which didn't fare badly in the comparison. I have many happy memories from the I.T. While there, I was appointed to work with Accord Carlow, the Catholic Marriage Care

---

* This article was a draft for a Silver Jubilee project for the Maynooth Class of 1991 that never advanced. Had that project proceeded, I am sure that John would have corrected the reference; Kildare played Louth in the first round of the Leinster Championship that day! It was Mick O'Dwyer's first Championship game as Kildare manager. This article was published posthumously in The Furrow magazine, November 2019

Service, and also took up a role with our diocesan services, later named the Faith Development Services. This offered great scope for involvement in pastoral initiatives in the diocese. In 2005, I was appointed curate in the Cathedral Parish, Carlow and in 2006 became administrator in that parish, where I'm constantly enthused by the deep faith and commitment of parishioners who seek to respond to the movement of God in their daily lives.

FAITH SUSTAINS

Faith itself has been the main sustaining factor of the last 25 years - the conviction that my life has meaning, that God has called me to something, even if it is not given to me to understand it. I've received immense strength from the Christian message itself, and so I have been surprised and disappointed at how people have rejected the Church because of the weakness and sinfulness of its leaders. Church leaders have always been weak and sinful - right from the time of Peter. The companions Christ chose abandoned him, and yet he sent these very people out after his resurrection to proclaim the good news. While they were transformed by their encounter with the Risen Jesus and by the coming of the Spirit at Pentecost, they still had to face the rest of the disciples, who knew that they had deserted Jesus in his need, who knew that Peter had denied him, who saw the disfunction of the 12 exposed in the betrayal and subsequent death of Judas. It can't have been easy. But the messenger is not the message. Society discredits the message because the credibility of the messenger is in doubt. The Church is not alone in this; it's how society works.

On the other hand, our message is about the Incarnation - the message takes flesh; it's meant to take flesh in us priests and in all Christians, so there's a validity in the criticism that points to the flaws in the messenger, for, like it or not, we embody the message. It makes you wonder about priests and our integrity as messengers of the gospel. What is our relationship with the message we bear? Is it clear? Do we value it? Is it real for us? If we don't value the message, how can we be messengers? Has our way of life lost its credibility? I remember years ago in seminary wondering if we were too comfortable, our lives not radical enough? In middle age, I'm much more comfortable than I was then, and Pope Francis, in his simplicity, challenges my middle-class comfort and lifestyle. As a seminarian, I remember a visiting priest, a Vocations Director from a diocese not my own, coming to Maynooth and asking the seminarian from his diocese who had arranged the room for him, to make sure he had two pillows, because as he said "after all he'd given up, it was the least he deserved." At the time, in my youthful idealism, I was horrified much to the amusement of the other seminarian, who still reminds me of it. I've always been of the view that because we have chosen this way of life, therefore we don't deserve anything. We are servants called to do our duty. However I find that more and more I'm slipping into the "two pillow-priesthood" - both mine, I'd hasten to add! People tend to insulate themselves with the comforts of life - small though they may be, and while there's nothing wrong with that and even the saints enjoyed their treats, we need to be careful that they do not insulate us from the radicalness of the call to discipleship and the mission that flows from it.

WHAT KEEPS US GOING?

So coming back to that question, what keeps me going on the journey? Many priests find that what is life-giving is in everyday parish life, in the experiences of the women, men and children who are part of our communities, who offer friendship and support and are open to the message that we try to bring. In sharing their lives, with all the ups and downs, we priests live life at its fullest and most meaningful, touching the very mysteries of existence as they enfold in daily life. Someone asked me once what was the source of my joy? The question surprised me, and my immediate thought was of my family who have sustained me - sometimes unknowingly - at some of the darker moments of ministry, particularly during the days after the Murphy Report. But the presence of the Lord has been even stronger.

The Italians have a prayer "May the joy of the Lord be your strength." It's a phrase I keep coming back to, and at times I use it as a mantra, and find that it lifts the spirit immensely. I believe that the source of our joy lies in our relationship with God. We might find great satisfaction in the work we do, great life and great hope in the people we work with and minister to, and many times of celebration and happiness, but the real lasting joy comes from our relationship with God. For us celibates, that is the primary relationship in our lives, and not just in our lives, it is the primary relationship in everyone's life. Our celibacy witnesses to that primacy in a unique way. But that witness means nothing if it is not real, if it is not lived, if the relationship that we claim to be the primary relationship is not in fact the primary relationship. May the joy of the Lord be your strength; it's so much easier to rejoice in the Lord when we know him. This leads us to the place that we give to our prayer. Prayer is about the time and space we give to God and that he gives to us. We preach about it to others;

we sometimes struggle with it ourselves. Sometimes it's good, but many times nothing happens. Yet it has the power to sustain us, to give us nourishment and meaning, and to bring us into the presence of the one who is the origin of all life and all love. Prayer is the place of complete honesty, where, like Adam in the garden of Eden, we cannot hide before God. He knows us through and through, and so here we find the place where we are known completely and yet utterly loved and accepted.

Two other phrases summarise much of what has inspired and energised me over the years. These are like mantras or mottos, phrases that have given me comfort, courage, enthusiasm and peace as they were needed. One is a version of Luke 23:46, a paraphrase of Ps 30:5,15, "Father, I place my life in your hands." This is the prayer of faith, of trust, confidence in whatever God might have in store for me, letting go and letting God. Belief in God's plan for us, in his love for us, in his providence removes an awful lot of the stress from life.

The other phrase is from psalm 26: "It is your face O Lord that I seek." This is about mission; it expresses the final destiny of humanity, to behold God face to face in the beatific vision, but it also expresses the mission to see the face of God in his people. It strikes me that our mission today is to be Veronica and to wash clean the face of Christ in today's world, to reveal the face of Christ in his body, the Church, where it has been sullied and is no longer visible to a lot of people. Here we are called to reveal Christ to the world in all his beauty and love. The call to seek the face of Christ in his people is a call to serve him in the people of our parishes and communities, and to seek him also beyond the safe confines of our churches, as Pope Francis reminds us. The good shepherd left the ninety-nine to seek the one who was lost; that one too bears the face of Christ whom we seek.

HOLY ORDERS

All Christians are called to exercise leadership in the Church, but in very different ways. Our baptism establishes each one of us as members of the Christian family, called to follow Christ, called to witness to him. The baptismal call is coming more and more into its own, and the leadership of lay people is finding both a voice and a means of expression.

Holy Orders, however, has always been seen as a particular gift that Christ has given, not to individuals, but to the Church. Priesthood is not simply about the priest, it's about the community he serves. A priest is one who answers the

4

call of Christ in a particular way, choosing to live the baptismal vocation, not in marriage or single life as most other people do, but in modelling his life on Christ and being united with him in a particular way of life, united with Christ through the sacrament of ordination, through a life of prayer, both personal and public, and through the ministry of service. I have always seen the priest as someone called to offer his life in union with Christ's; he is the one who says on behalf of Christ during the Eucharist "this is my body, given up for you." Saying these words at Mass challenges me to make them my own. While they echo the call of all Christians to give their lives for others in imitation of Christ, nonetheless it is the priest who follows the example of Christ in offering his life for all; it is the priest who says those words in the liturgy on behalf of Christ, and so is called to witness to them in a distinctive manner. Priestly celibacy is a particular expression of that offering, made not to one person, but for the community.

The task of proclaiming Christ is more urgent than ever before. Since the election of Pope Francis, whose patron was entrusted with the rebuilding of the Church during a mystical experience in Assisi, a new period in our history is beginning. Our world is crying out for hope and for meaning. Our Church needs new vision and energy. It still needs shepherds who will lead God's people into union with him, shepherds who will uncover the holiness of God's people and reveal the face of God. Jesus points towards his unique relationship with the Father when he says, "The Father and I are one". But it is also the goal of our life in Christ. We are called to union with God, and there is a crying need for priests who will witness to that call in their own lives and lead people towards it in their ministry. Stephen Covey's "7 Habits of Highly Effective People" was very popular a few years ago. One of the habits he suggested was to begin with the end in mind - in other words, have a goal and keep it in sight. In the busyness of life, we might forget that we're pilgrims on a journey and our journey has a destination. We're destined for union with God - that's the goal, the proclamation of it is our work and our life. In some measure, we seek to achieve and experience that union already in our communion with God and with one another. Evangelisation is part of the journey; the Kingdom of God is the goal. Keeping that goal in mind is important every day because not only does it remind me that I'm not alone, but also allows me to keep a sense of perspective about my life and its relative unimportance - I'm part of the picture, not the whole picture - that's Christ. I don't always have to get it right - God will use our failures as well as our successes. For me, it's important just to be on the journey.

When I was a child, my mother used to say our prayers with us in the mornings before going to school. She always began with the Morning Offering. She told us not to say "I offer you all my prayers, works and sufferings", but rather "I offer you all the prayers, works and sufferings of this day" because then, not only were you offering your own life, but everyone else's as well, so that everything you did and everyone else did would be a prayer. If you followed her logic, well then you might never need to utter another prayer for the rest of your life!

But I took to her logic pretty well, and that notion of offering the whole day, my whole life, was part of the daily routine and fed into my vocation as a priest. It was very eucharistic, and it made a big impact on me, firstly as a child, when I thought it was a great way of doing an awful lot of praying with very little effort. But as an adult, I found in it the roots of a Eucharistic spirituality, where in the bread and wine offered on the altar, we offer also all that they represent - fruits of creation representing the entire creation, work of human hands, telling of all that is human, so that the preparation of the gifts becomes something more than just the preparation of the bread and wine, but the presentation of life, creation and all that is human, in its joy and hope, anguish and sorrow. All of it is offered to Christ, all of it is transformed, all of it becomes a new creation, the sign of the transformation of all in Christ, when God will be all in all.

Here in the Eucharist, all of life comes together. Each person comes with an individual story; each comes to touch and to share the life of God. But God is not afraid to touch our lives and to share them. He knows our stories, so we are not afraid to acknowledge our human frailty and to allow God to touch our vulnerability as we express our need of his loving kindness. Then as a people united in his presence, we take our part as the heavenly liturgy unfolds in our presence.

We are nourished, challenged, healed and uplifted by the proclamation of God's word, through which Christ becomes present to us. We remember the offering of Christ in his death and resurrection, made present now in bread and wine. The new covenant breaks in among us, rupturing the heavens and disclosing Christ's presence with us, while foretelling creation's final union with

God. Here in the gathering of the Christian people to celebrate the mystery of Christ's love for us, everything comes together as one. This is the place of unity, the place of nourishment, the place where God's people are fed on the journey even as they anticipate the banquet at journey's end. I usually lose people when I start to talk about the Eucharist, but I find that this approach helps me to make sense of life and faith, bringing them together in one place and one point. Writers such as Pierre Teilhard de Chardin, Jean Corbon, Jeremy O'Driscoll and Paul McPartlan have coloured much of my thinking.

EUCHARIST AND THE CROSS

We don't talk much about the cross these days - I'm reminded of a bishop who visited the chapel of a diocesan seminary a few years back and as he looked at the books on the pews, saw the modern book covers of contemporary authors and he wondered at the spiritual reading of the seminarians and said: "Where's John of the Cross? Where's Teresa of Avila? All I see are sand-dunes and palm-trees!"

I'm all in favour of sand-dunes and palm-trees - but that's for holidays. Real life is tough. A teacher in school used to say to us, as he piled on the homework, "Life is hard, lads!" I haven't forgotten that lesson: life is hard. The cross is part of life, whether we like it or not, and it's part of the story of the Eucharist, present in the crushing of the grain and grapes, present in the offering of Christ on the cross. I received an ordination invitation which had, on its cover, an image of the priest superimposed on the crucifix, sharing the cross with Christ. It spoke of a spirituality that isn't too popular today. But we have to get to grips with the cross. We cannot put it to one side; we cannot avoid it; we cannot deny it. Because we know that we've been there too. We've been the body of Christ hanging on the cross, and we may well be in the future as well.

This really excites me about our worship. I'm convinced of Christianity and its truth because of the way that it faces the hard realities of life - suffering, evil, death. Without denying any of them, it offers a meaning and a way forward. God sent his Son among us, not to give us answers, but to be with us - he is Emmanuel, God with us. And God-With-Us lived with us, suffered with us, died with us, showing us that this is how life is. It's tough and it's rough, and we mightn't understand it - and he didn't seem to understand it very well either in Gethsemane - but we're not alone. He is with us. Christ didn't give us answers but he stood by us and suffered with us, and, in fact, went one step further than we do - he went beyond death and revealed to us the new life of the Resurrection. This un-dreamed of revelation transforms our approach to suffering, not by denying its reality, but through its transformation. Christ gives us no answers, but he shows us the way. Critics of Christianity would talk of the "pie in the sky when you die" spirituality, but it's more about solidarity while you live, knowing Christ is present with you in your suffering. Finding him, placing your hand in his and trusting in the darkness that he will guide us to the fullness of life. The resurrection may even, at times, seem like too much to hope for, but it is the ultimate affirmation and vindication both of the physical body and of human suffering. Created in God's image and likeness, our bodies are fleshed spirit, and so are destined for eternal life.

EUCHARIST AND VOCATION

For me, the Eucharist is at the heart of priesthood. Here is where Christ offered his life, giving us a ritual so that we can participate in his gift of his life on the Cross. It's a privilege to say the words of Christ "take this, this is my body, which will be given up for you." I always feel these words are at the heart of all Christian vocation and all Christian life, where we are called to give our lives in love, as Christ gave his. In marriage, the husband and wife say these words to one another - "this is my body, my life which I give for you"; their life as a Christian married couple originates in this moment, as Christ gives his life to the wife and to the husband in and through each other, nourished and energised by the body of Christ whom they have received, living in them, giving in them, uniting in them. As priest, I say those words, not directly to anyone else, but in the person of Christ, who said them as he gave his life for all. As the person who says those words of Christ on his behalf, I have to make them my own by giving my life for all. My saying these words brings me right into the gift of my life that I am asked to make, the vocation that I am called to follow. These words inspire and nourish my life as a celibate, bringing that part of my life right into the heart of the Eucharist, endowing it a meaning and an energy which keep me going when the day to day living out of celibacy brings its challenges and struggles.

In giving our life, we imitate Christ who washed the feet of the disciples. This is the other great symbol of Eucharist, the diakonia, or service that is the essence of Christ's self-gift. This is my body given for you...it's for others, for their sake, for our sake, that Christ gave his life, and many beautiful things have been written about the washing of feet over the centuries. So much of our lives is given to the service of others; diocesan priesthood holds that balance between the service of washing feet and the more contemplative offering of bread and wine. The strength of priesthood is not in power, but in service; it lies in the washing of feet. The beauty of priesthood is the face of the Risen Christ revealed in us, for us, and through us. We've been formed to see ourselves as alter Christus, 'other Christs', acting in persona Christi, in the person of Christ. Along the line however, we may have forgotten that it is Christ whom we serve in his people. It is the face of Christ that we see in the faces of our parishioners and others. Often priests have been so preoccupied with their calling to be alter Christus that we have forgotten about the Christ whom we serve in the person of the other. Thus, as well as telling stories of generous self-sacrifice, genuine love and inspiring holiness, the history of the priesthood also tells a tale of arrogance and pride, self-absorption and resentment. Obviously these aren't compatible with priesthood, but they are evidence of the 'earthen vessels' which God uses to hold his precious gifts.

Most of all in the Eucharist, I am sustained by the presence of Christ himself. In the frailty of bread, he gives himself, uniting himself to us in a way that is so simple, yet almost beyond belief. To carry within us the presence of God and act as his tabernacle - this is mind-blowing stuff. But when you consider that in receiving Eucharist, we are not simply Christ-bearers, but are united with him because we are fed with him, then we are truly in a space beyond human comprehension. At the end of life's journey is the union with God, theosis, which we can only imagine. But it begins here, through the medium of bread and wine, as we are called into the communion of one body - communion with Christ and with one another, a union with the Church present at the Eucharistic celebration, a union with the Church of all ages, a union with the Church of heaven, a union with Christ, in his living, dying and rising. And so, the very mystery of Christ's life becomes part of us and part of our lives, as we are caught up into the eternal presence of Christ.

CONCLUSION

A description of the priest that has always made sense to me is Interpreter of Life. We are there to help people make sense of their lives, particularly at the key moments - birth, marriage, illness, death, bereavement, trauma, experiences of meaninglessness, hopelessness, poverty, need, but also helping them to understand and appreciate love, joy, hospitality, sharing, caring. We are interpreters of the mystery of life, helping people to get a glimpse of God's presence, if not his plan, in their various life experiences. It's our privilege as diocesan priests to be living at the frontiers of life, the places where life is on the edge, as we struggle to push the boundaries of meaning and belief, hope and love, courage and endurance, and lead our people into faith. We're more than ministers of the rites of passage who provide a pleasant background for secular celebrations; we endeavour to lead people into the heart of what those celebrations are truly about; to open their eyes to perceive God's presence; to open their hearts to welcome his love; to open their minds to the deeper wisdom and understanding of the Spirit of God at the critical junctures.

The Church faces many challenges in Ireland today; some of these are political, concerning the credibility of the Church in society etc, but the deeper crises are spiritual. Irish people still are deeply aware of God's presence but are not confident in responding to that awareness in the Church and so search for it elsewhere. Priests need to be sensitive to their searching, and aware too of the richness of the Christian tradition of meditation, mysticism, retreats and holistic spirituality. We need to enhance our ability to articulate that tradition. We also need to be confident in the message we proclaim, and to be able to sit with those who struggle with the Church and to dialogue with them. It's an exciting time to be a priest, a challenging time, one that offers new opportunities for mission and evangelisation. Hopefully we're neither too tired nor too demoralised to embrace these. Ultimately, it is comes down to our confidence in God's ability to use us to achieve his purpose, whatever that purpose might be - to let go and to let God. In the words of St. Paul, Glory be to him, whose power, working in us, can do infinitely more than we can ask or imagine. (Eph. 3:20)

While the history of the Church in Ireland over the past 25 years has been pretty dismal, consisting of revelations of scandals, depravity and mismanagement, one might be philosophical and observe that life has always been difficult. Each age brings its own challenges; that's life and the Christian life points to the cross as a constant presence, no matter when we may live. The challenges of our time are ugly, not just because of their unpleasantness, but because they reveal the presence of evil in the heart of the Church and because so many of them are largely of the Church's own making. The scandals of sexual abuse are part of a wider picture of abuse within society which society still fails to confront. Being a priest during the time when these scandals have been uncovered has not been easy and at times you want to escape from it, particularly when you are aware of unfair comment or clergy bashing. We're an easy target. But Christ came to suffer for the guilty and we must share that part of his mission too. So many innocent people suffer when some commit a crime. Their family and friends are affected and so too is the circle which surrounds the perpetrator, his family, friends and colleagues, no matter what the crime.

I used to think that the Church influenced the culture and society of which it was part; now I wonder if the culture of the Church stems, in fact, from the culture of the time, and if it is society which creates the dominant ambiance within the Church rather than vice versa. After all, Church people grow up in families and communities and are moulded in them before ever making an adult commitment to religious life. It's an interesting thought, but one that might too easily let the Church off the hook.

YEAR A

ADVENT AND CHRISTMAS

First Sunday of Advent[12]
Waiting in Joyful Hope

I'm often intrigued by the prayer we say after the Our Father, "Deliver us, Lord, from every evil." It ends with the words "as we wait in joyful hope for the coming of our Saviour, Jesus Christ." I sometimes wonder – do we? Do we wait in joyful hope for the coming of the Lord? Have we any consciousness of waiting for him to come again? Or if we think about it at all, is it something we'd prefer not to be around for? Is there any bit of "joyful hope" in our waiting? Is there any bit of joyful hope in us at all?

Advent is all about joyful waiting; it begins with our looking forward with joy to the coming of Christ again. It moves towards the welcoming of Christ who comes into our lives and into our hearts now, again and again each day; and it finishes as we celebrate the birth of Jesus, who first came into the world as a new-born babe in Bethlehem 2000 years ago.

That attitude of joyful hope contrasts with the sense of foreboding and fear that is present in the gospel today. Jesus speaks of the coming of the Son of Man as a time of judgment; it will come suddenly, and unexpectedly, at a time that no one can know. The Lord will come like a burglar, like a thief in the night. However, this shouldn't worry us; we are called to stand ready for him, to welcome him. There's an urgency about the second reading too, as St. Paul calls on the Romans to live in readiness for the coming of the Lord; we are people of the light; we are to live in the light, and to emerge from the darkness. The Old Testament reading from the prophet Isaiah paints a most beautiful picture of the gathering of all peoples at the mountain of the Lord. This is what we long for; the coming of the kingdom

'So stay awake, because you do not know the day when your master is coming... Therefore, you too must stand ready because the Son of Man is coming at an hour you do not expect.'

Mt 24:42,44

For personal reflection

Listen in the silence of your heart for the Son of Man who visits daily.

13

of God, a place and time where swords will be hammered into ploughshares and spears into sickles; there will be no more war, no more hatred. The final call of Isaiah is similar to the call of Paul and to that of Christ "House of Jacob, come, let us walk in the light of the Lord." These images appeal to the idealist, the dreamer in us all. We long for the peace that the coming of Christ promises. In the turmoil of our world, we cry out to him to come. In the times of turmoil in our own lives, we recognise our need of him; in our despair and in our confusion, in our grief and in our guilt, we crave his presence; we hunger for his peace.

This evening we light a candle on the Advent wreath, the first. Our streets are already festooned with Christmas lights. And soon our homes will also be filled with sparkling lights and candles too, as Christmas comes. Perhaps you will light a candle on Christmas Eve and place it in the window to welcome the Christ Child. The birth of Christ is the coming of light into a darkened world. And all these signs; all these lights, all the candle-lighting rituals mean nothing if they do not symbolise the longing of our people for their God. Of course, many will say that they mean nothing anyway. But for us who watch for him, for us who recognise the needful yearning of this world and its people for its Saviour, - for us, these lights are filled with meaning and hope. For us, these lights are the sign of our joyful hope. When he comes, will he find us watching for his presence? Or will we be too busy rushing around, stressed and tired? The world we live in is just as much in need of a Saviour as it ever was. He has come; he still comes, and he will come again. He still brings light where there is darkness, hope where there is despair, joy where there is none. Let us welcome him. Let us be the sign of his presence; let us wait in joyful hope for the coming of our Saviour.

[1] Isaiah 2:1-5
     Psalm 121(122):1-2,4-5,6-9
     Romans 13:11-14
     Matthew 24:37-44
[2] Homily given on 2 December 2007

SECOND SUNDAY OF ADVENT[34]
PREPARING THE WAY

At the moment it feels like it's been Christmas for a month already. I've seen decorations in homes as well as in the shops and streets; it seems to get earlier every year. There's a sense of busyness and bustle about, as people do their shopping and make their preparations. With all tinsel and glitter and the sparkling lights, I fear that we will have exhausted our Christmas energy before it even begins. Will we even recognise that it's Christmas when it comes? Perhaps society is still celebrating the ancient pagan festival of Saturnalia, but with a Christian gloss.

Underneath the urgency and frenetic activity that forces Christmas on us earlier and earlier, there's another layer of preparation, where the focus is on Christ. We Christians are preparing for Christmas in a season of waiting that we call Advent, a time that looks for Christ's coming. We open our eyes afresh to his coming among us now in the day-to-day matter of our lives; we look forward with hope and expectation to his second coming, and we celebrate with joy his coming among us as a human being, born 2000 years ago. The candles of the Advent wreath mark our patient waiting. Three of them are purple - this is the colour of preparation, the colour of repentance.

Looking at the gospel today, we see John the Baptist also looking for the coming of the Christ, the Anointed One, the Messiah. The man he's looking for is very different to the sentimental Christ that our society celebrates. In stark and uncompromising terms, he calls on the people to repent, to turn away from sin and to turn to God. The One who is to come, he says, will clear his threshing floor and

This was the man the prophet Isaiah spoke of when he said:

A voice cries in the wilder-ness: Prepare a way for the Lord, make his paths straight.

Mt 3:2

FOR PERSONAL REFLECTION

How are you preparing for the Lord?

gather his wheat into the barn, but the chaff he will burn. Strong words, putting the urgency of repentance upon us.

To repent is to turn around, to face a different direction, to look to Christ. Advent is all about looking to Christ - looking to Christ especially when we're distracted by the excess with which we celebrate Christmas today and find ourselves buying into it - literally. We have always found that this is a good time to go to Confession - to clean the house as it were, to welcome Christ once more; it's about leaving the darkness and facing the light. No one likes going to Confession; very few of us want to own up to our own sinfulness. I don't like going to Confession, but I know that it keeps me focused; it keeps me on the right road.

Confession is not just about confessing our sins - that's not the most important part of it really; it's about celebrating the mercy of God, welcoming it right into our hearts, experiencing what it is to be forgiven. Many people have chosen not to come to Confession; others have simply lost the habit - and it's a good habit. Don't be afraid of it; the diocese issued a leaflet about going to Confession earlier this year, and you might find it helpful - it outlines what happens in Confession and explains a bit about the sacrament. If you didn't get one in the Spring, you might like to take one now.

Prepare a way for the Lord - make his paths straight. There are lots of crooked paths in all our lives that need straightening out; all of us need to prepare a way for the Lord. Consider how best you might do that this Advent time.

---

[3] Isaiah 11:1-10
       Psalm 71(72):1-2,7-8,12-13,17
       Romans 15:4-9
       Matthew 3:1-12
[4] Homily given on 4 December 2016

THIRD SUNDAY OF ADVENT[56]
JOY OF EXPECTATION

Sharon and Carmel are two popular female names, both of them from places in the Holy Land, known for their beauty. The Plain of Sharon is a wide expanse of land north of the biblical city of Caesarea, while the mountains of Carmel are just to the north. Today in the first reading from the prophet Isaiah, their splendour is evoked, as it proclaims the glory of the Lord. The Lord is coming; the wilderness is alive with flowers and growth; all of nature is rejoicing; the weary are encouraged; the blind will see; the deaf will hear; the lame will walk; sorrow will be ended, and there will be only joy, an outpouring of joy at the coming of the Lord. The Messiah ¬will come and will bring a new era, an age of peace and prosperity for all, a time of healing and harmony. In the gospel, we see Jesus pointing out these Messianic signs to the followers of John, who wondered if it were true – has the Messiah come? Yes, he says, look at the signs and see for yourselves.

This third Sunday of Advent – Gaudete Sunday – is the day when traditionally the joy of expectation bursts through our liturgy, and we celebrate the coming of the One who is already here. For in Advent, we watch for the coming of Christ again, the second coming, when all things will reach their fulfilment, their destiny, their judgment. Next week our focus is very much on celebrating his first coming, 2000 years ago in Bethlehem. Today we recognise that he comes to us here and now, each day of our lives. Every day is Christmas; every day is the coming of the Messiah.

But where then are the signs of his coming? Where are the signs of his presence in our lives?

Go back and tell John what you hear and see; the blind see again, and the lame walk, lepers are cleansed, and the deaf hear, and the dead are raised to life and the Good News is proclaimed to the poor; and happy is the man who does not lose faith in me.

Mt 11:4-6

FOR PERSONAL REFLECTION

Take time to feel the gift of JOY in your life today.

There is such an amount of suffering; the blind, the deaf, the lame, the weary – they're still with us. If Christ comes every day; if he is present in our world, why is there war? Why is there suffering? Why is there so much hatred?

When we look at how Jesus came into the world in Palestine 2000 years ago, we get a glimpse into how he comes into our world today. He came in poverty, unnoticed, unheralded. The rejoicing that Isaiah foretold did not happen in the way it was expected. There were many blind and deaf and lame who were not healed. Many people came to him, listened, and turned away. Nothing has changed. Many didn't come at all. One of the great crosses that Jesus had to bear was not on Calvary, but during his ministry, as he faced the pain of rejection by his own people. He comes into the world today, offering to heal the blindness and deafness in our lives, offering to open us to something better, something more, and we reject him; we turn away. I do and we all do. The world rejected him the first time, and it still rejects him today. It's almost as if we're afraid that in accepting him as fully as he accepts us, we will have to give more than we want.

But we don't always reject him; time and again, he comes into our lives, and we let go of our petty concerns, our resentments, our anger, our hardness of heart. We invite him in, and we truly experience joy; we are really alive. The joy of the Lord is our strength. I'm always amazed not that God comes to my rescue when I need him most; but I'm always amazed at how he comes to me, not as I expect, not as I want, but nonetheless he comes. Sometimes he comes with healing; sometimes he comes with good news; sometimes he invites us to share his cross; sometimes he wants to share ours. But even in difficult times, he brings joy – not the joy of bubbles and effervescence, but the joy of the Lord, difficult to describe, but one that goes with being at peace with ourselves, with others, and with the world. In this Advent season, let us welcome the One who comes. Let us open our lives to celebrate his coming into our lives, not just at Christmas, but today and every day. May the joy of the Lord be our strength.

---

[5]   Isaiah 35:1-6,10
      Psalm 145(146):6-10
      James 5:7-10
      Matthew 11:2-11
[6]   Homily given on 16 December 2007

Fourth Sunday of Advent[78]
Importance of a name

When a new baby is expected, one of the things people wonder is "what will the child be called?" Our name is so important; not only does it distinguish us from everyone else and give us an identity, but it can also be something that causes people to make judgements about us. We get certain ideas about people from their name, ideas which may or may not hold water. The naming of Jesus was done by the angel before ever he was born. Two names are given for him: Jesus, which means "God saves," and "Emmanuel" which means "God is with us." These two names identify the baby born to Mary; they tell us who he is and what the purpose of his life will be. We are told that the name "Jesus" is given because this child is the one who will save people from their sins; Emmanuel reminds us that, in him and through him, God is present with us; he is God's presence with us.

As we approach the feast of his birth, I wonder have we any sense of needing him at all? One of the things you hear said often enough is that there was too much emphasis on sin in the past, and we should steer away from it, and instead emphasise the goodness of people. Perhaps. But this child came among us to save us from sin, and if there is no sense of sin, do we need him? Do we need a Saviour if there's nothing to be saved from? I would suggest that perhaps our idea of sin was perhaps at fault; perhaps we misunderstood what sin was and therefore were filled with a misplaced guilt. Because you have only to look at the headlines in the papers to realise how badly our society needs to be saved from sin, how much our Church needs to be saved from sin, and indeed we don't have to look beyond

The virgin will conceive and give birth to a son, and they will call him Emmanuel, a name which means 'God-is-with-us'.

Mt 1:23

For personal reflection

Do you have a sense of needing Jesus?

19

ourselves to realise that sin is present in us too. We are a sinful people, a sinful Church, a sinful community; we say and do things that are selfish or hateful or unkind; we can be neglectful and dishonest and so on, and it is only by the grace of God that we can rise from that.

The Good News is that God sent his only Son to save us from sin – he is Jesus – the one by whom God Saves. It is in the place where we fall and are broken that he meets us; it is in the realisation of our weakness that he is our strength; it is in the experience of our humanity frailty that we can discover his saving mercy. The place of repentance is the place of grace. Our world can often be an ugly place where people do ugly and cruel things to one another; it needs a Saviour and so do we. And God has already sent us that Saviour, so that as we journey through life, our experience of his mercy and forgiveness draws us closer and closer to him, even without our knowing it.

So, we should never despair at our shortcomings or our misdeeds. Sadly, many people do, and they are filled with feelings of inadequacy and self-hatred. No matter how bad we feel we are, God is with us – Emmanuel; he is with us as one who loves us and never abandons or deserts us. He it is who will save us and lead us into a place where we have a proper sense of love for ourselves as the beautiful creatures that God has made in his image and likeness. It is no accident that we celebrate Christmas at the darkest time of the year; it is no accident that the infant Son of God was born in the darkness of the night. That is where he is needed most; that is why he came – to be a light wherever people experience darkness in their lives, to bring the light of love and forgiveness to the darkness of sin and blame, to save his people from their sins.

---

[7] Isaiah 7:10-14
   Psalm 23(24):1-6
   Romans 1:1-7
   Matthew 1:18-24
[8] Homily given on 18 December 2010

Christmas Day[910]
We need these days of celebration

Today is a day of light and joy and celebration; today we celebrate in a way that is completely over the top, the birth of a little baby. We celebrate with gifts, all wrapped colourfully and Santa Claus (hope he didn't come too early); we celebrate by giving to those in need; we celebrate with special food. We celebrate with songs, carols, games; we celebrate with other people; we celebrate with joy. When he was born, the party wasn't quite what it is now, but there was still singing, by angels in the night sky; there was a special light, a star; there were gifts brought by the wise men a few days later. But it was all very obscure, all very local. A little baby, born in a stable to a poor couple - who'd have thought that we'd remember him today?

We need these days of celebration. It's no accident that we celebrate Christmas at the time of the year that is darkest - the heart of December. We look to Christ, the light of the world, to come into the darkness that is all around and to be light in those places. We know all too well the brokenness of our world; every year we seem to discover new levels of unhappiness, new avenues of suffering and pain in our own land and throughout the world. Today we acknowledge our need of a Saviour, our desire for a Saviour, our thankfulness that the Saviour has come.

We could simply celebrate Christ's birth as an anniversary - a day to remember that this is when Christ was born. But to do that would be to miss the meaning of Christmas. Christmas isn't simply for remembering a birthday; it's about celebrating a birth and what that birth means. It's about allowing Christ to be born once more in our lives, a time for renewal, a time to make a home for Christ in our own life and in our hearts.

And suddenly with the angel there was a great throng of the heavenly host, praising God and singing:

'Glory to God in the highest heaven, and peace to men who enjoy his favour.'

Lk 2:13-14

For personal reflection

Allow Christ to be born once more in your life...

When he was born 2000 years ago, Jesus was born in a stable because there was no room in the inn. But this story is more than about homelessness. Stables are places where we keep animals, they're not always clean places; they can be smelly; they can be dark, perhaps cold. We all have those places in our lives - the dark, cold places of our hearts, the ones that are smelly and dank, places we don't like to show to other people. That's where Christ wants to come this Christmas; that's where he needs to be born. That's why the Church puts a big emphasis on Confession, so that we can open the doors of our dark places to Christ and allow him to enter in - the light of the world, the healer of hearts, the giver of life, the source of forgiveness and love.

As Christmas day progresses, the readings change at each Mass - last night we had the story of his birth. This morning it was about the coming of the shepherds. Now that they've gone home and the stable is quieter, there's a bit of reflection going on - what does all this mean? Who is this child? No less than the Word of God, the second person of the Trinity, the One who has existed since before the beginning. "The Word was made flesh; he lived among us." This is what we celebrate - God is on our side; God is with us. There is no darkness too great for him. He comes to share our life, from its fragile beginning to its end. He comes to be with us in our joy and in our sorrow. Because God has become human, something new has happened to creation; something new has happened to humanity. In our brokenness and our pain, in our smelly stables and dark places, the Son of God has come among us. This is the time of light, of hope and of joy.

Look on this child in the crib and see the Saviour. Look at him with hope and recognise our salvation and the salvation of our beautiful and suffering world; let us look at him with love and follow him in the year that lies ahead.

---

9 Isaiah 9:1-7
   Psalm 95(96):1-3,11-13
   Titus 2:11-14
   Luke 2:1-14
10 Homily given on 25 December 2016

Feast of the Holy Family[1112]
We still see family at the heart of society

It was lovely on Christmas Eve and Christmas Day to meet so many families come together for Christmas; there were stories shared about long journeys and difficulties coming home, and great joy in being here to celebrate this great feast of family. One young man from abroad was unable to get home due to the airport closures and was delighted to be spending Christmas here in Carlow, as he said "with a family."

As we know, the nature of family and of family life has changed considerably over the years. Once the unit was the extended family, with grandparents, uncles, aunts, cousins and the whole web of relationships held in unity; in more recent decades, the nuclear family unit took prominence, and more recently again, we have far more diverse family structures in society. Whatever the make-up of the family may be, we are still a society that sees the family as being at the heart of society. Families are important.

As we come to celebrate today the Feast of the Holy Family of Jesus, Mary and Joseph, the gospel story we have heard puts some interesting themes before us – the safety of the family, migration and emigration, themes which have returned to prominence in Ireland. In the days of the Celtic Tiger, many families came to make their home here for economic reasons and reasons of safety and security. Many who were refugees, like the Holy Family, now live at home here. In latter days, we have seen families and family members leave these shores to seek their fortune elsewhere. Another outstanding issue in the gospel is the role

May the peace of Christ reign in your hearts; let the message of Christ find a home with you.

Col 3:15,16

FOR PERSONAL REFLECTION

Give thanks for your Christian family and pray for them daily.

of the father. Joseph is very prominent in this story; in this story, he is the protector, the guardian and guide of his family, charged with leading them to safety and protecting them from the danger that threatens. His situation invites us to consider the role of fathers in families today. Certainly, that role has changed over the years. The tasks of protecting the family and also of protecting the young have been among the most prominent topics in our society in the last number of years. These issues, in all their many facets, look likely to preoccupy us well into the future.

But also in this Christmas season, we are reminded that at the heart of the family is the presence of God. Today we're called to recognise this, to cherish God's presence and to develop our awareness of his love and his presence in the life of the family.

We are invited to recognise also our own membership of the family of God: the holy family that is the Christian community, the body of people who call God their Father and Jesus their brother.

---

[11] Ecclesiasticus 3:2-6,12-14
Psalm 127(128):1-5
Colossians 3:12-21
Matthew 2:13-15,19-23
[12] Homily given on 26 December 2010

Feast of Mary, Mother of God[1314]
We honour Mary, the God bearer

The passing of an old year and the beginning of a new one is often a time for nostalgia, for looking back and for looking forward. For most people, the New Year brings hope, optimism about the future. It's a blank canvas and can mark a new beginning. It can be a time for thanksgiving, with gratitude for the blessings of the past year. But it can also be a time when we are glad to see the end of a difficult period in life and look forward to something different and new. For some, it's a time of darkness and fear, as they dread the continuation of their problems into the future. Every year brings its own challenges and we rise to meet every year in the freedom and hope of the children of God. We have been gifted with so many gifts, love, strength, courage and many others. Most of all we have been given the gift of God's Son and the Holy Spirit, so that in every day of the year, we are never alone. We walk in the strength of the Spirit, in the presence of Emmanuel, God with us.

The Church celebrates two things on New Year's Day. On the one hand, it is the feast of Mary, Mother of God. You might wonder why we begin the year with a feast dedicated to Our Lady, not to Christ, but that's to miss the point. The title we give Our Lady today is Mother of God; that title was itself the cause of one of the great controversial divisions in Church history - is Mary the Mother of God, or just the mother of the man Jesus? If that's the case, is Jesus two persons, one human and one divine, united in one body? or is he one person with two natures, human and divine? - this led on to the question of the very salvation of humanity - if the Son of God is not truly Son of Mary, then he cannot be truly human? and if he's not truly human, that places our salvation in jeopardy. All very complicated. The resultant debates and councils confirmed that Jesus is fully human and the title Theotokos, or God-bearer was given to Mary, Mother of God. And so, this day is

As for Mary, she treasured all these things and pondered them in her heart. And the shepherds went back glorifying and praising God for all they had heard and seen; it was exactly as they had been told.

Lk 2:18:20

FOR PERSONAL REFLECTION

Ponder peace in your heart and be part of the solution.

25

really about a reflection on the meaning of Christmas as we enter a New Year. We enter this year full of amazement and joy because God has sent his Son among us, born the Son of Mary, fully human and fully divine, two natures, but one person. We enter this New Year, with wonder and awe that God has become human, and has therefore changed what it means to be human forever. The way to God has been opened for us as never before. God became human that humanity might become divine. We enter into this New Year with confidence because Jesus is with us, God with us, and Mary, his Mother is our Mother also.

The second thing that the Church celebrates on New Year's Day is World Day of Peace. We're asked to observe this day as a day of prayer for peace, a time to ask for God's peace in our own lives and situation, and throughout the world. We're very conscious of the global turmoil which has engulfed our world. Many people are also fearful for the future. Today we're invited to turn to God once more with confidence and trust.

The story of the shepherds coming to the stable makes the whole Christmas story a bit more human and colourful. Like many a wise man, they had been watching, reading the signs, and it was the sign in the night-sky, the angels and their message that led them to the stable at Bethlehem. From there, they went out and told others what they had seen and heard, and their story caused astonishment.

At the heart of the scene is Mary, quietly listening and treasuring all these things and pondering them in her heart. Mary's serene presence is hard to fathom, so soon after giving birth. But her contemplative spirit is depicted here; she had not just welcomed God's Son into her womb and given birth to him, she had also welcomed him into her heart and he still remained there. She had no idea what lay ahead; here she was in a stable with her new-born baby, soon to flee into a foreign land. Uncertainty lay ahead. She is calm and trusting, full of faith, aware that God is with her, even though she might not understand his plan or its implications. Her gentle confidence might well serve us for this coming year. Like her, let us welcome the presence of the Lord into the very heart of our being. In the turmoil of the times we live in, let us trust in the One who sent his Spirit upon a young girl in Palestine and chose her as Mother of His Son. May he, the Good Shepherd, lead and guide us in 2017.

---

13 Numbers 6:22-27
Psalm 66(67):2-3,5,6,8
Galatians 4:4-7
Luke 2:16-21
14 Homily given on 1 January 2017

SECOND SUNDAY AFTER CHRISTMAS[1516]
OUR FAITH IS THE SOURCE OF LIFE, ENERGY AND LOVE

Here we are at the beginning of another New Year. Some will see it as a new beginning, a time for hope, a time for bidding goodbye to the worries of last year and a chance to look forward to the promise of a new year, with all that it might bring. Others might be a bit more subdued. However, the gospel today brings us back to the beginning; here at the start of a new year, it is fitting that we look right at the beginning of all. It gives a sense of perspective and puts both our hopes and our worries into context.

"In the beginning," we are told in the Prologue to St. John's gospel, "was the Word; the Word was with God and the Word was God. Through him, all things came to be." These words govern all that follows in scripture and in life. If we do indeed hold these words to be true, then God is the fundamental reality, the basic truth of life and of everything. Everything we are, or know or do, comes from this divine source. Our faith is not just the framework within which we live and work, but it is also the source of life and energy and love; there is nothing else: "not one thing had its being but through him." And so today as we set out in this New Year, we remember our ultimate beginnings, the origin of our life in God, and this recollection hopefully will inspire us, literally, filling us with the Spirit, and will stay with us throughout the year ahead.

We're still in Christmas, reflecting on the birth of God's Son, mulling over its meaning, pondering its significance, wondering at it. At the start of a new year, a little bit removed from the exuberance of the Christmas celebrations and even from the sentiment of the crib, - what does it mean – that

The Word was the true light that enlightens everyone...

Jn 1:9

FOR PERSONAL REFLECTION

Give thanks for your Christian family and pray for them daily.

27

God took human flesh and was born as one of us? Does it mean anything? Does it change anything? Are there implications for us? For many, it changes nothing, and they continue to live as if nothing had happened. But for all of us, it should change everything.

Emmanuel. God-is-with-us. Even as we must struggle and seek for ways to cope with the economic situation, knowing that God-is-with-us must help. What we do cannot leave God out. Recently people have shown great care and kindness to others, e.g. during the bad weather, contributing to good causes, giving to SVP... That sort of generosity is not just for Christmas. There is no substitute for good neighbourliness and human friendship.

This time of crisis is an opportunity to build an economy in which profit and growth are at the service of people, an economy which brings benefit to all our people, thinking especially of children, the elderly and the most vulnerable.

In helping each other, there is hope.

The Prologue of St. John's gospel also acknowledges the darkness that is part of life. Christ, the Word of God, comes as the light to a world in darkness, a light that the darkness cannot overpower. For us, this is the source of our hope. We share in that light through baptism. ... May we not contribute darkness through anger or greed.

All other lights, including the lights of poetry and art and music and even our own light, are merely reflections of this light, the true light of the world. Our task is twofold – firstly it is to discover the light of Christ for ourselves, to allow Christ to be light for us, and secondly it is to reflect that light for others. Let that be our resolution for 2011 – to let Christ be light for us and in us, and through us then, may he be light to the world.

The Word became flesh and lived among us; this is the heart of the Christmas message. The Word became flesh and lived firstly as a little baby, and then grew up to be a man 2000 years ago. This man, God made flesh, gave his life for us, and continues to give his life for us in bread and wine in the Eucharist, the ritual he left us to re-present his presence among us. So today, through the bread and wine of the Eucharist, Christ takes flesh in our flesh; we incarnate his presence today. In the darkness of this world, we are to be light. But we can only be light.

During the week, I heard a discussion on the radio about the places in which people might find hope in 2011. The arts were mentioned prominently, as places where truths could be articulated and understood, where music, poetry and art open our minds to something bigger, something beyond the darkness which many experience. I found it interesting that neither faith nor religion was mentioned as a place where this hope or opening to the transcendent might be uncovered. It's a sign of the times, perhaps.

---

[15] Ecclesiasticus 24:1-2,8-12
   Psalm 147:12-15,19-20
   Ephesians 1:3-6,15-18
   John 1:1-18
[16] Homily given on 2 January 2011

FEAST OF THE EPIPHANY[1718]
JESUS - A LIGHT THAT SHINES IN THE DARK

The account of the Epiphany is a great story – wise men following a star in search of a new-born king, another king with evil intent, a baby born in a stable, and then gifts with special meaning. It all adds up to a great story. However, it was never just a story; it's part of the account of the events surrounding the birth of Jesus which is deeply symbolic and points towards his identity and his role. He is king who comes in humility not in majesty; he is a light that shines in the dark; he is one who is recognised, but not by many. Those who honour the child come from afar. Today is often remembered as the feast of nations, the revelation or epiphany of God's Son to the world, which is represented by the wise men.

One of the details of the story that fascinates me is how the wise men recognised the star as it rose and followed it. It was probably regarded as an act of madness. A star is a light in the night sky; it gives a certain radiance, but the light of one star seems small and insignificant among all the other stars of the sky. This star leads the wise men to a baby; again, this is a small and seemingly insignificant person, powerless and weak, without wealth or position. How can this be the great king that they expect?

I'm struck by the contradictions present in our stories of how Jesus Christ appeared in the world. Even the Old Testament readings speak of him as the light of the dawn, the rising sun. The rising sun is not the noonday sun; it appears in the darkness of the night; it promises that the day is coming and the darkness is at an end, but that promise, while it is certain, is not yet fulfilled.

The sight of the star filled them with delight, and going into the house they saw the child with his mother Mary, and falling to their knees they did him homage.

Mt 2:11

FOR PERSONAL REFLECTION

Reflect on the stars in your life that bring you great delight.

And so with Christ; he comes as a little light, born into an insignificant little country, with a message that brings the certain promise that the darkness of the world is over and that the light of day has come. But the darkness is still present. We still have to search for the light, and it's easy to miss it or even to dismiss it.

In our own time, people still search for the light, still search for truth. Not all of them find the star that leads to Christ; not all of them see his light and his promise or recognise it for what it is. We ourselves can find it difficult to understand and to perceive, especially when the darkness of life seems stronger. In times of worry and trouble, in times of grief or hardship, in times of recession or illness, or family difficulty, in times when the darkness seems to invade our very being, we wonder if it is true.

Is Christ the light of the world, and if he is, why do I not see it? Why does he not deliver us from the dark? Why?

There is a tension which is part of Christian belief, a tension between our faith in the Christ, the light who has come into the world, our deliverer and redeemer, and our experience of a world that is still in darkness, still in need of light, still searching and looking for meaning and for redemption. It is the tension between the rising sun and the dark of night. The sun is here and the coming of the day is sure and certain, but the night is not yet gone, and we still live with the darkness. The challenge for us is to have confidence in this new light, the light of Christ, the courage to follow his star, even though its light may seem small, even though the darkness may be profound. Like the wise men, let us have the courage to put our faith in the light which came into the world through the birth of a child in Bethlehem.

---

17 Isaiah 60:1-6
   Psalm 71(72):1-2,7-8,10-13
   Ephesians 3:2-3,5-6
   Matthew 2:1-12
18 Homily given on 6 January 2011

For some reason, this Christmas I've been drawn to the image of the stable again and again. It seems such a lonely, dark place, a dank cave away from the warmth and welcome of people's homes and the hospitality of an inn. Being a place where the animals were kept, at the very least it smelt of their smells. Yet this was where God chose for the birth of his Son. Right from the outset, Christ is with the outcasts; he's with the animals, outside the house in the dirt and the darkness because this is his mission - to seek out the outsider, to bring light and healing to the dark, dank places of peoples' lives, to cleanse what is unclean and let all who feel unloved and unwanted know that they are indeed God's children. We might consider the stable to be the image of human sinfulness, our need of salvation.

The feast of the Baptism of Jesus always occurs on the Sunday after the Epiphany. It marks the beginning of the adult life and ministry of Jesus, and it's an event that perplexed the first followers of Jesus, as, like John the Baptist, they struggled to understand why he chose to be baptised by John and not the other way around. John baptised sinners as a sign of repentance; people came to him, responding to his call to turn away from sin and wrong-doing and to open the way to God. Jesus had no need of this baptism, but here, right at the beginning of his ministry, he stands with sinners. He walks with those who know the darkness in their lives and seek the light. This is another stable, a place where the Son of God is in solidarity with the desperation of humanity, enthralled to darkness and the stench of evil, and coming to be washed clean, to enter the light. This is the Christ who came to offer himself

And a voice spoke from heaven, 'This is my Son, the Beloved; my favour rests on him.'

Mt 3:17

FOR PERSONAL REFLECTION

Welcome Jesus into your heart, into your life, into your brokenness and into your sin. Come Lord Jesus, Come.

for sinners, the One who today still gives his Body and Blood for the forgiveness of sin.

The images associated with human sinfulness are ugly and sometimes frightening. The reality of evil is even worse. We see the plight of those who suffer on our screens, victims of warfare, refugees, victims of terror, of hatred; we have seen too the callousness of those who commit crimes against humanity. It's easy to point out the global wrongdoing. But the conflict between good and evil goes on in every human heart. Each one of us needs to be saved. Each one of us needs a Saviour. Christ comes at Christmas into the stable that is my heart, my life, my brokenness, my sin.

Christ was baptised in the Jordan with me and for me, just as much as for anyone else.

The total solidarity of Christ with humanity is obvious from the very moment he appears in public; his action in accepting baptism from John testifies to the mission that he is called to fulfil - to undergo a different baptism, one which would deliver humanity from sin and death into the fulness of life - this was the baptism of the Cross, his suffering, death and resurrection. The voice of the Father is heard today proclaiming Christ as his Beloved Son, also foreshadowing the new relationship that humanity is called to with the Father. Christ today embraces his own humanity and ours as well, in all its beauty and in all its brokenness. Today he signals the journey that he will make, giving himself for us sinners, and rising from death to lead us into a new relationship with the Father. Christ comes to break the power of evil in the world, so that all people can live as children of God, for all are called to know his love and forgiveness. He comes to establish a new relationship between humanity and God. Let us give thanks today for the baptism which we received which has united us with Christ and given us the promise of this new life.

---

[19] Isaiah 42:1-4,6-7
    Psalm 28(29):1-4,9-10
    Acts 10:34-38
    Matthew 3:13-17
[20] Homily given on 8 January 2017

YEAR A

SUNDAYS IN
ORDINARY TIME

Following directions and getting lost was a bit of a theme for me during the week. A friend of mine came to visit last week and took the wrong exit from the motorway, and so entered Carlow on the Wexford road, and got completely lost trying to find the Presbytery. Eventually they phoned and someone went to meet them. But earlier in the week I took a wrong turn myself in Dublin after being at a meeting there, and the signposts sent us astray, and it took a bit of patience to find our destination. It's always important to have the right directions; it helps too when you follow them. But we've all probably gone astray at some stage due to a signpost pointing the wrong way.

John the Baptist is often compared to a signpost; he directs us to Christ; he points him out to us; he is his witness. This is his role; this is what he was chosen for. Last week we celebrated the baptism of the Lord; today John points out to us its significance. This is who Jesus is: The Lamb of God, the one who is to be offered up for all. We say those words at every Mass; Lamb of God, you take away the sins of the world.... And so, the role of Jesus is also highlighted for us. John's role is to be a signpost, pointing towards Jesus; Jesus' role is to take away the sins of the world, to be offered up as the spotless lamb who will carry the sins of the people; he is the Chosen One of God; he is the One on whom the Holy Spirit came down. The first reading develops the role of Jesus a little bit by describing him as the servant of God; in Hebrew the word for servant is similar to the word for lamb. This servant of God according to the prophet Isaiah is the one who will restore the

Seeing Jesus coming towards him, John said, 'Look, there is the lamb of God that takes away the sin of the world. This is the one I spoke of when I said: A man is coming after me who ranks before me because he existed before me. I did not know him myself, and yet it was to reveal him to Israel that I came baptising with water.' John also declared, 'I saw the Spirit coming down on him from heaven like a dove and resting on him. I did not know him myself, but he who sent me to baptise with water had said to me, "The man on whom you see the Spirit come down and rest is the one who is going to baptise with the Holy Spirit." Yes, I have seen and I am the witness that he is the Chosen One of God.'

Jn 1:29-34

FOR PERSONAL REFLECTION

What are the sign posts you were presented with by God regularly?

Were there sign posts you missed recently?

peoples to the Lord and bring them back to him; his task is to be light to the nations, and to bring God's salvation to all.

Roles are important in the second reading as well. Paul tells us that he has been appointed by God to be an apostle, and the role of the people of God is indicated also – they "are called to take their place among all the saints everywhere who pray to our Lord Jesus Christ; he is their Lord no less than ours", says Paul. Here in the first month of the year, we are reminded that our role, our call is to take our place among the saints, to be a people of prayer, united with Christians throughout the world, and all who worship the same God.

During the week we heard of the plans to beatify Pope John Paul II next May; this means that he is on the third step to being made a saint. It recognises that he has entered heaven and can intercede for those who pray in his name. It takes place after a miracle is recognised which has been achieved through the intercession of the person. The decision to beatify Pope John Paul was fairly rapid; after all he died only five years ago, but that rapidity is not unknown. Others have been beatified and even canonised within a year or two of their deaths, although it doesn't happen as often in modern times.

The journey to sainthood is something to be taken seriously; we say perhaps we're not holy joes; we can be afraid of being seen as too holy or religious or pious, as if that would in some way diminish our credibility. But what kind of credibility have we got in the eyes of the God who calls us to be saints. The path to sainthood will be quite different for each one of us; we have different lives; we pray differently and have different spiritualities; our faith encounters different challenges, but we are on the same journey. Pope Benedict reminds us again and again that we are called to be saints. In the glory days of the Celtic tiger, our country saw itself as a shining light for the world economies; that light now appears to have given false hope. It has certainly dimmed. But if we are to be a light for the nations, as Isaiah says, then we should be a light of truth, light of love, a light aflame with the presence of God. Our faith is not something static, not simply a belief that we hold and that's the end of it. It's about our relationship with God, about growing in that relationship, discovering the beauty and joy of the Lord as we come to know him closer;

it's about witnessing to the presence of God as we journey through life. Perhaps we can take heart from John the Baptist who tells us twice in the gospel that he did not know Christ, did not recognise him, but through his listening to the voice of God, he came to recognise him. We too need to listen to the voice of God and to respond to it, so that we too might take our place among all the saints everywhere who pray to Jesus Christ.

---

[21] Isaiah 49:3,5-6
Psalm 39(40):2,4,7-10
1 Corinthians 1:1-3
John 1:29-34
[22] Homily given on 16 January 2011

Third Sunday in Ordinary Time²³²⁴
Called to lead

It's been a momentous week. The British Prime Minister spelled out the implications of Brexit for Britain and Europe; the Northern Ireland Assembly was dissolved, and elections called; and Donald Trump was inaugurated as President of the United States of America. It was an interesting week, to say the least, and many people feel that it marks the beginning of a new period of uncertainty for society. Of course, all the other things that are contributing to uncertainty continue - the unrest in Syria, the ongoing refugee crisis, the battle over Catholic values in Ireland - it all goes on. There are some today who will hear today's readings and see them to mean that after years of darkness, light has come to the world in the form of Brexit, Donald Trump and all the other changes that have come about. Others might be of the opinion that more than ever, we still walk in darkness and need the light of Christ, the light of God's love to guide and sustain us as we tread these unknown paths.

As I reflect on the gospel today, I wonder what it says to us now. We see Jesus at the start of his mission fulfilling the prophecy of Isaiah as he appears as a light for a people in darkness, preaching and calling his first four disciples. His first followers were four fishermen. Two of them were actually fishing when Jesus asked them to drop everything; they were earning their living, providing food for themselves or to sell to someone else. I wonder are the ordinary things of life distracting us from something more significant. The other two were mending the nets with their father. Did you ever think that our world, maybe even we ourselves, might be caught in a tangle of nets, trapped in the complexities of day to day life and the issues and problems of today, so that we don't

From that moment Jesus began his preaching with the message, 'Repent, for the kingdom of heaven is close at hand.'

Mt 4:18

FOR PERSONAL REFLECTION

Take time this week to listen to the many ways God is calling you in faith.

hear Christ when he calls; we don't see him, and we don't respond. Certainly, there are times when I feel that I'm tangled up in the nets myself, and it's not easy to get sorted out.

The call of Christ to follow him is not a new one; we've heard it before. Or we've heard the words, but have we really heard the call, heard it so that it resonated with us deep down in our hearts. His call comes together with an appeal to 'repent', in other words to turn around and face a new way. I wonder if we are locked into a vision of life that is too narrow, too limited. I was reading yesterday about two Germans who were executed during the Second World War, Edith Stein, a German Jew who became a Carmelite sister, was gassed at Auschwitz and is now canonised as St. Teresa Benedicta of the Cross and Dietrich Bonhoeffer, a Lutheran Pastor, who was executed at Flossenburg Prison. Both of them had a deep awareness of the need to turn radically to Christ, to offer their lives to him, and to strive to live the Christian way more fully, more deeply. It's not just that we're asked to follow Christ, but firstly we're asked to repent, to turn to him and leave behind the things that hold us back from living authentic Christian lives. Bonhoeffer wrote of the dangers of cheap grace, grace without repentance, grace without discipleship, grace without the cross, grace without Christ.

Whether we are married or single, widowed or priests, religious or engaged, young or old, we are called to follow Christ in a radical commitment that involves turning around and looking at him, facing him - in other words, repentance, in its original meaning, metanoia, turning and facing a new way. It means leaving the things that entangle us, the nets that ensnare, sometimes even leaving people who are important, our livelihood. How we follow Christ is unique to each one, but in the world we live in today, with all the serious issues it faces, we must take our discipleship very seriously if we are to play our part in the building of God's kingdom in a changing, uncertain environment. Not everyone is a Peter or an Andrew, James or John. Some are Zebedees, keeping the boat afloat, playing their part, letting their sons go, doing the normal things. To paraphrase Mother Teresa of Calcutta "we cannot all do great things, but we can do small things with great love."

---

[23] Isaiah 8:23-9:3
 Psalm 26(27):1,4,13-14
 I Corinthians I:10-13,17
 Matthew 4:12-23
[24] Homily given on 22 January 2017

FOURTH SUNDAY IN ORDINARY TIME[526]
MISSION STATEMENT FOR LIFE

One of the characteristics of agencies, groups, businesses in our society today is that many of them have a mission statement or a vision statement. A vision statement is about how the group sees itself and what its values are; a mission statement is more focussed on the purpose and objectives of the group. Both within the Church and in society as a whole, this kind of statement is used to help particular groups focus on their identity and their aims as they go about their business. They tend to be inspirational statements. The gospel reading today – the beginning of the Sermon on the Mount – could perhaps be said to be a vision statement for the kingdom of God. If you can imagine bringing the beatitudes into a meeting in your workplace or even into your home and asking, "is this what we're about?" Or even to say, "if this is really what we're about, how are we making it happen?" Vision statements are challenging; they remind us what we're called to be; they put our highest ideals in front of us. When we're content to survive from day to day and from deadline to deadline, vision statements, if we choose to look at them, dare us to lift our heads from the mundane and to question whether our day to day reality corresponds to the vision.

The beatitudes have inspired Christians and non-Christians for centuries. Do they inspire us? "How happy are the poor in spirit; theirs is the kingdom of heaven." These are the people who know their hunger for God, people who have realised how much we need God, how much we depend on him. Many in our society do not experience that need; they're not in touch with it, for one reason or another. They cheerfully live their lives with little reference to God. Where do we stand?

'How happy are the poor in spirit; theirs is the kingdom of heaven.

Happy the gentle: they shall have the earth for their heritage.

Happy those who mourn: they shall be comforted.

Happy those who hunger and thirst for what is right: they shall be satisfied.

Happy the merciful: they shall have mercy shown them.

Happy the pure in heart: they shall see God.

Happy the peacemakers: they shall be called sons of God.

Happy those who are persecuted in the cause of right:
theirs is the kingdom of heaven.

Mt 5:2-11

FOR PERSONAL REFLECTION

Reflect on the ways you have felt the loving and caring hand of God in your day.

"Happy are the gentle." Our society has become very aggressive; when we get annoyed, we let off steam. How often do people get angry with others on the phone, in shops, in businesses? Gentleness and meekness stand out when we meet them.

"Happy those who mourn." We find it hard to recognise sometimes how God stands close to us in times of sorrow and difficulty. But it's good to know that he cares, that those who suffer are not abandoned, that bereavement and loss are not his last word. Those who mourn will be comforted.

Then we have those who hunger and thirst for what is right. They're the ones who do God's work, the people who make his vision for the world a reality. They look for justice and recognise the value of every person, of our earth, and are not afraid to strive for it.

"Happy are the merciful." The teaching of Jesus really emphasises mercy; our society today is much more concerned with retribution, sometimes even confusing retribution with justice. The way of Christ is the way of forgiveness, the way of kindness to those in need. This challenges our generosity of spirit, particularly if we have been wronged.

"Happy are the pure in heart." Integrity is a wonderful quality, perhaps the most difficult of all, as it suggests a unity between our beliefs, our values and our way of life, something that hopefully we strive for.

The peacemakers build unity and harmony between peoples; there's often one person in the family or in the workplace who is particularly good at this. But we are all called to be peacemakers, to seek peace in our own lives and to offer it to others as well.

The final two beatitudes speak of those who are persecuted in the cause of right and those who are abused and persecuted for Christ's sake. We may feel that we're carrying the martyr's palm when we suffer in the wrong. But all too often the one who is wronged becomes an aggressor, as the demands of damaged pride and anger and vengeance make themselves felt. Jesus turned the other cheek. And this, he says, is the way to real happiness.

Next Wednesday we begin the season of Lent, the Christian season of repentance and renewal. We may have already chosen a particular way to observe the season. We may be quite indifferent to it. In the past, the rules about observance of Lent were very strong, so that it was quite obvious that people were observing it. In recent times, the onus and responsibility for Lenten observance is on the individual. We choose what we do. And I wonder if it would be worthwhile taking the Beatitudes as a theme for Lent, as our vision statement, to really reflect on them and to try and live them, maybe choosing one of them each day and reflecting on its meaning for our lives. In returning to this Christian vision statement and truly seeking the vision they put before us, our experience of Lent would contribute immensely to our spiritual growth.

[25] Zephaniah 2:3,3:12-13
   Psalm 145(146):6-10(Lord6)
   1 Corinthians 1:26-31
   Matthew 5:1-12
[26] Homily given on 3 February 2008

One of the great themes of the Second Vatican Council was the role of lay people. The Council opened the way for lay people to become involved in Church and parish in many different ways, and it highlighted the tremendous significance of the sacrament of baptism, the first and fundamental sacrament upon which our whole vocation as followers of Christ is based. Pope Francis, in common with all the Popes of recent times, is very conscious of the role of the baptised and seeks to encourage and support lay people in it. At its heart is the call to build up the kingdom of God; we are all of us called to be witnesses to Christ, and to work for his kingdom in the world today. The transformation of the world in the social, political and domestic spheres is at the heart of the role of the laity. Lay people are called to witness to God's presence and to build up his kingdom, wherever they are, be it at home, at work, at leisure - wherever they might be. Today our culture tries to tell us that religion and faith are private things, and we can feel and be made to feel awkward in sharing them. Not so. Today Christ tells us that we are salt for the earth and light for the world. Light is only of value where there is darkness. 2000 years ago, Christ recognised the darkness that was present and called on his followers to be the light.

Being Christ's light does not mean that we're continually talking about faith, or preaching in an overt way, although sometimes that might be helpful. In a phrase attributed to St Francis of Assisi, we should preach always and sometimes use words. Usually it's about who we are, our attitudes, our values, the fact that we're not afraid to say or do the right thing, that we're not afraid to mention

Jesus said to his disciples: 'You are the salt of the earth. But if salt becomes tasteless, what can make it salty again? It is good for nothing, and can only be thrown out to be trampled underfoot by men.

'You are the light of the world. A city built on a hill-top cannot be hidden. No one lights a lamp to put it under a tub; they put it on the lamp-stand where it shines for everyone in the house. In the same way your light must shine in the sight of men, so that, seeing your good works, they may give the praise to your Father in heaven.'

Mt 5:13-16

FOR PERSONAL REFLECTION

How am I a light in the darkness for others?

Think of the ways you are preaching always and sometimes using words.

God, to talk about Christ. It's about values and attitudes that are rooted in Christ and built on him. There's no point in privately believing in something and having particular values unless we do something about them; that's the equivalent of hiding our light under a bushel.

Christ does not just call us the light of the world; he calls himself the light of the world. The light we give is not something that is just of ourselves; it's not simply about sharing our gifts and talents and letting our light shine. It's something more profound. It's about allowing the light of Christ to shine in us and through us; it's about being his witnesses, channels of his love and grace, his instruments in the world today. The light does not shine so that people can see the light; it shines so that they can see clearly. It's not about us, it's about helping others to see clearly, to perceive the truth, to live clearly, to know Christ.

There's a lot of darkness in the world today; the darkness of hatred, oppression, violence, fear. Some of them are outside our scope of influence. But there is darkness in our own society too, poverty, prejudice, anger, addictions. It's easier to take a stance on some of these than on others. But where are values are conflicting, it's not so easy. It's not easy to know what is the darkness and what is the light, particularly where conflicting rights and responsibilities are involved. At those times, we need to be even more Christ-centred and Christ-focussed, so that our values and opinions are shaped by him and not by self-centredness or convenience.

At our baptism we are brought into relationship with God, a relationship that is key to the rest of our lives. We are the place where God makes his home, the dwelling place of the Spirit. The Spirit does not invade our space, but comes gently, shaping us and moulding us in ways of forgiveness, tenderness and love. When we are filled with the Spirit, filled with his light, it is then that we are most truly ourselves. As we nourish our friendship with the Lord and grow in his ways, may we also bear witness to his truth and his love, so that his light may shine in us and enlighten the hearts and minds of all people.

---

[27] Isaiah 58:7-10
  Psalm 111(112):4-9
  1 Corinthians 2:1-5
  Matthew 5:13-16
[28] Homily given on 5 February 2017

Sixth Sunday in Ordinary Time[2930]
Setting attainable standards

For the last few Sundays the gospel has been from the Sermon on the Mount. It's a long sermon, a collection of the teachings of Jesus, which goes on for three chapters in St. Matthew's gospel, chapters 5, 6 and 7. We're still on chapter 5. And we hear some of the moral teaching of Jesus, his teaching about how we are to live, the rules we should observe. They come across as pretty strict; in fact two things are noticeable. One is that, this is a far cry from the gentle, kind Christ who soothes us and consoles us - here Jesus is challenging us, setting a standard. The other thing you might notice is that Jesus is setting a higher standard than the one that was there before. He says "You have heard how it was said....., but I say to you....." He claims an authority for himself to set a standard higher than the one Moses set, and so puts himself before Moses. In fact, he's claiming the authority of God, and that would have been a real challenge to the powers that be.

We sometimes feel that Jesus is so loving and caring, and that he so understands our human nature, that we're not being held to as high an account. When the question is asked, "what would Jesus do," there's a tendency to choose the most compassionate response and to let the principal or command slide a little. Yet here, Jesus is calling us to set the bar higher than it ever was before. The first reading today reminds us of our freedom which enables us to choose to do what is right, in spite of how we might feel. "If you wish, you can keep my commandments; to behave faithfully is within your power." We might blame temptations, companions, our own human weakness - but actually the ability to choose the right thing - to live faithfully is within

Jesus said to his disciples: 'Do not imagine that I have come to abolish the Law or the Prophets. I have come not to abolish but to complete them.

'For I tell you, if your virtue goes no deeper than that of the scribes and Pharisees, you will never get into the kingdom of heaven.

Mt 5:17,20

For personal reflection

Reflect on the phrase "to behave faithfully is within your power" In the quiet, take five minutes to write down the ways you have chosen to behave faithfully AND note the God given fruits of those choices.

our power. We are free; not only are we free, but we are graced by God, given the Holy Spirit, who brings gifts of wisdom, understanding, right judgement - all of which help us to make the right decisions and to reject what is wrong.

We live in a season of Mercy - last year was the year of Mercy, and Mercy is the hallmark of Pope Francis' papacy. Our compassion for one another when we fail, our concern for those who cannot reach the standard set by Christ, the mercy characteristic of the followers of Christ - none of this should compromise or be compromised by the standards that Christ has set. We don't change the rule because it's difficult and people find that they cannot live with it; nor should we be found wanting in forgiveness and care for those who don't or can't reach the standard that Christ has set. This is what we aim for - a community with values that are based on truth and compassion as partners working together.

One of the teachings of Christ that people sometimes find difficult is his teaching on marriage. At a time when divorce was permitted in Jewish Law, Jesus raised the standard and called people back to the Father's original plan for marriage - that it is a life-long commitment between man and woman. Those whose marriages are in crisis or have broken down need and deserve all the support and compassion that a Christian community can give. Pope Francis recently streamlined the annulment process to speed it up and help those who seek the freedom to remarry. You might like to let people know about that and to encourage them to explore that process, if remarriage in the church is something that they would like to do.

---

[29] Ecclesiasticus 15:16-21
   Psalm 118(119):1-2,4-5,17-18,33-34
   1 Corinthians 2:6-10
   Matthew 5:17-37
[30] Homily given on 12 February 2017

Someone said once that the sad thing about Christianity is that it has never been tried. I'm not sure about the truth of that, but when you consider the gospel we've just heard, you might be tempted to agree. Today Jesus comes to the nub of his moral teaching: the call to go further, to give to the point that it hurts, to love your enemy, to pray for those who persecute us. This is raising the bar to a level that seems unattainable. Right throughout the Sermon on the Mount, Jesus is raising the bar for us. Over the last 4 weeks we've been reading chapter 5 of St Matthew's Gospel, the first part of that famous collection of Jesus' teaching, which began with the Beatitudes, and each week, the gospel message has been more challenging than the one we've heard the week before. Jesus took the law of the time and put a new one in its place - one that challenges us to love in a new, deeper way, a way that will eradicate all self-love and self-centredness, self-pity and fear of the other. The old law said, "an eye for an eye", Jesus says, "offer the wicked no resistance." Evil cannot be fought with evil, only with love, and any resistance we offer needs to come from love, not hate. When we confront, we do so in order to transform or enlighten them, not knock or malign them down; it is in turning the other cheek that we are to call wrong-doers to repentance, revealing their wrong to them and inviting them to a change of heart. Love your neighbour and hate your enemy is replaced with love your enemy.

Perhaps the reason that we fail so spectacularly to live out the admonitions of Jesus in the Sermon on the Mount is that we tend to view his teaching as simple morality - dos and don'ts,

'You have learnt how it was said: You must love your neighbour and hate your enemy. But I say this to you: love your enemies and pray for those who persecute you; in this way you will be sons of your Father in heaven, for he causes his sun to rise on bad men as well as good, and his rain to fall on honest and dishonest men alike. For if you love those who love you, what right have you to claim any credit? Even the tax collectors do as much, do they not? And if you save your greetings for your brothers, are you doing anything exceptional? Even the pagans do as much, do they not? You must therefore be perfect just as your heavenly Father is perfect.'

Mt 5:43-48

FOR PERSONAL REFLECTION

God loves us with an extraordinary love, and he wants us to truly receive that love and to share it with others.

Reflect on your personal journey. Is your journey filled with acts of love and kindness to others and welcoming the God who comes to you in love.

and we find them simply too difficult. How can it be possible to love our enemies? Or else we see them as impossible standards - something that's there to inspire us, but not really attainable. Maybe they're unrealistic; maybe we're just not able to reach that standard. In some ways, it would be cruel to set an unreachable or impossible standard before us, and the scriptures tell us that it is possible to live the commandments as Christ taught us. Perhaps it's about remembering that Christianity is not just about rules and morality, not even primarily about rules and morality, although at different periods in our history that's where the emphasis has been. Christianity is first and foremost about relationship. Christ became human, lived among us and brought us into a new relationship with God.

In baptism, we become God's children, called to relationship with God who is our Father, Jesus who is our Brother and Saviour, and the Holy Spirit, who comes and lives within us. From that relationship of love, we are called to observe the teaching that Jesus gives. And we do not do it on our own, no, we live and we love in the presence, the strength and the power of the Holy Spirit, dwelling within us. As St. Paul reminds the people of Corinth, at a time when many of them were leading immoral lives, "Didn't you realise that you were God's temple and that the Spirit of God was living among you?...the temple of God is sacred, and you are that temple." We are called to love others heart and soul; we are called to return good for evil, love for hatred, forgiveness for hurt and wrongdoing, because God is love and we live in God and God lives in us. We live and love, not with our own strength and love but with the strength and love of God present in us. So let us stop and pay attention to the presence of God within; let us listen and feel and intuit how God is moving in us and in the events of our lives. That's what prayer is about - stopping and becoming aware of how God is present and living and active within us. If we live in God, then we will live in love.

---

[31] Leviticus 19:1-2,17-18
Psalm 102(103):1-4,8,10,12-13
1 Corinthians 3:16-23
Matthew 5:38-48
[32] Homily given on 19 February 2017

Eighth Sunday in Ordinary Time[3334]
Dealing with addictions

Over the last two weeks the children who are preparing for Confirmation have had the opportunity to hear the stories of some people who are recovering from addictions in Cuan Mhuire treatment centre in Athy. We know only too well the suffering that addiction can cause not just to the person who suffers from the addiction, but also to family, friends and those around them. Every now and then, we see programmes on television which tell some of those stories. Unfortunately, in Ireland we have a real problem with addictions; we have a traditional and ongoing problem with alcohol. Changing attitudes is much more difficult and more important than anything else, because that's where the key to changing behaviour lies. As a community, it's up to all of us to help foster responsible attitudes to alcohol, as well as supporting young people to enable them to resist the pressures of peers, their natural curiosity and the attraction of alcohol or drugs. Today, Temperance Sunday, is the day when our candidates for Confirmation here in the Cathedral usually take their Confirmation pledge. It's always the Sunday before Lent begins, and it offers us an opportunity to reflect on what a difference Lent might make for us. Do we need to make a pledge of some sort for Lent? Do we need to abstain from something? Lent is not about tokenism - it's a chance for real growth, a time when we can do serious work on ourselves and on our faith-life.

Part of the journey to Confirmation involves taking the pledge to abstain from alcohol. The young people make different commitments, some choosing to abstain until they are 18 or 21, others making a particular commitment to their

Jesus said to his disciples: 'No one can be the slave of two masters: he will either hate the first and love the second, or treat the first with respect and the second with scorn. You cannot be the slave both of God and of money.

Mt 6:24

FOR PERSONAL REFLECTION

Looking back on your day, were there times you felt you a slave to the things of this world? How did you repair this and turned your focus back to GOD?

parents and guardians. All of them are asked to promise to abstain from dangerous drugs. One of the reasons the pledge is part of the journey to Confirmation is that these young people are growing up and beginning a process of growth into a more adult world which will take them through their teens and into their twenties. As they grow, they need to foster mature attitudes and to be protected from what they are not yet able to handle. The tradition of taking the pledge at Confirmation is a distinctly Irish one, with roots in the Pioneer Movement, founded by a Capuchin priest, Fr. Theobald Matthew [sic]. The children will be given the opportunity to be part of that association, if they choose.

For the boys and girls today, this stage in their preparation for Confirmation is a reminder that following Christ is about the way we live our lives, by the witness we give, the discipline of our life as disciples of Jesus. In the gospel, Jesus calls on us to trust in him, to trust God. We are loved by God with a love that is unimaginable. God wants only what is good for us; he wants the best for us. He asks us to seek always what is good; to seek his kingdom first and his righteousness. To abstain from drugs for life and from alcoholic drink is very real gesture and an outward sign of our commitment to Christ; we pray that God will give the girls and boys the grace and the strength that they will need to keep their pledge, particularly in those times when other people are encouraging them to take a drink or to try drugs. They will need courage and strength and the presence of God working in them.

---

[33] Isaiah 49:14-15
   Psalm 61(62):2-3,6-9
   1 Corinthians 4:1-5
   Matthew 6:24-34
[34] Homily given on 26 February 2017

One of the things you become conscious of in a society such as ours is the shakiness of the foundations of so many of our institutions. I don't know if it's simply the recession or the signs of a society in decline, but there's very little you can take for granted, and very few of the traditionally rock-solid bodies have emerged unshaken from the turmoil of recent years. The worlds of religion, finance and politics have been shaken and found wanting. Now they struggle to rebuild, to start again, to find more solid ground on which to build and so learn from the errors of the past. For religion, and especially for our religion, that means coming back to Christ and recognising where and how we have failed to listen to his teaching and follow his way. And it is not an exaggeration to say that in some ways the Church has parted company with Christ in the past; the Church is a human institution, albeit one with a divine element as well, and like all human realities, it is prone to sin and failure, and all the foibles that characterise the human world. In his letter to the Irish, Pope Benedict has called us to turn again to Christ and to begin the renewal of our faith and our Church by building on him and on his teaching.

This is the very thing that Christ calls us to do today in the gospel; he warns against the very dangers that have shaken the faith of so many people today. A faith and a Church that are not built on Christ will be swept away by the rain, the floods, the gales of our time. On the other hand, if our foundations are strong, if our faith and our Church are rooted in Christ, then we have some chance of withstanding the challenges that come.

What is true for the Church is true for us as individuals also. What is our faith based on? Is it a

'Therefore, everyone who listens to these words of mine and acts on them will be like a sensible man who built his house on rock. Rain came down, floods rose, gales blew and hurled themselves against that house, and it did not fall: it was founded on rock. But everyone who listens to these words of mine and does not act on them will be like a stupid man who built his house on sand. Rain came down, floods rose, gales blew and struck that house, and it fell; and what a fall it had!'

Mt 7:24-27

For personal reflection

What is your faith based on?

Ask yourself how it relates to Christ? Reflect on the insights his teaching give?

Does your faith refer back to Christ?

Christ-centred faith? I was talking to someone the other day about spirituality and we commented that for many people today spirituality is about many things, but Christ and religion are not necessarily among them. As Christians, we are called to build our spirituality on Christ; to be rooted in him, planted in him, built on him. He is our rock, the stronghold of our faith. To centre our spirituality on Christ is not to suggest that our spirituality be any way narrow or limited, for Christ is not limited. But it should refer back to him as the centre. If we are going to explore other spiritualities, spiritualities based on insights and practises from the eastern traditions, spiritualities or practises focused on Mary, spiritualities and practises inspired by the cosmos and the earth, or simply a spirituality that is based on love of neighbour, then let it refer back to Christ. Ask how it relates to him, what insight does his teaching give in this approach? What light can he shed on it? And how does this spirituality reflect his presence? Where is he in it?

We are Christians, followers of Christ. Christ is our rock, no other. There are many ways to know him, many paths to approach him, and they can all be very helpful. But it is to him that they should lead us, not to some other place, where we can find easy comfort. Christ's path is not always easy; it involves the cross, it demands trust, and it is characterised by love. We are called to build our lives on him, and we do this by listening to his word, welcoming it, reflecting on it, pondering it, letting it take root in our hearts and bear fruit in our lives; we build on Christ when we welcome him in the Eucharist as the bread of life – bread, that thing of everyday, that is so essential to human survival. Here he nourishes us, strengthens us, and here we are invited to recognise and welcome him in a unique and deeply personal way. We build on Christ as the rock when we turn to him in prayer and call on his name and make space for him in our lives. We build on Christ as the rock when we recognise his presence in the world, in the love of others, in the glory of nature and the beauty of the world. We build on Christ as the rock when we see him suffering in the faces of the needy, the ill, the old, and those in distress and respond to them in love and compassion. If you don't know how to build on Christ, then ask him to show you how. Lent is starting next week. This is a time to build, to rebuild, to fix the broken bits of our lives and our faith as we prepare for the great festival of Easter.

---

[35] Deuteronomy 11:18,26-28
Psalm 30(31):2-4,17,25
Romans 3:21-25,28
Matthew 7:21-27
[36] Homily given on 6 March 2011

YEAR A

LENT AND EASTER

First Sunday of Lent
Master or slave?

One of the visible signs that Lent has begun is the way we wear ashes on Ash Wednesday; it's a very ancient practice, a continuation of the sackcloth and ashes of the Old Testament, a sign of repentance, and a reminder of our mortality. But it's only a token, a reminder, a simple sign. We live in a time that needs more than tokens, we need action; we need change based on reality. Lent marks that period during which we, as Christians, renew our lives. There should be no tokenism about it. Anything we do, in terms of our prayer, fasting or almsgiving, is done with a goal in mind – the renewal of our lives in Christ, the rooting out of bad habits, the starting again. Long ago in the fifth century, Pope Leo the Great spoke of this as a time to struggle with temptation: He said,

"Whatever steps forward we make, there is not one of us who is not always bound to do better. All of us must strive hard and so on Easter day no one should remain bound by the vices of his former nature. And so, dearly beloved, what every Christian should always be doing must now be performed more earnestly and more devoutly. These forty days, instituted by the apostles, should be given over to fasting which means not simply a reduction in our food, but the elimination of our evil habits."

His words are stark, and they call on us to set forth on a journey of pruning that will lead to growth. The readings today convey that same sense of starkness. The origin of the problem of evil is recounted in the book of Genesis as the story of a couple, Adam and Eve, and how they are led astray by a serpent. The serpent manages to convince them that what is forbidden is good and desirable, that taking it will result only in positive consequences. The result is that their eyes are opened to the reality

Jesus was led by the Spirit out into the wilderness to be tempted by the devil. He fasted for forty days and forty nights, after which he was very hungry, and the tempter came and said to him, 'If you are the Son of God, tell these stones to turn into loaves.' But he replied, 'Scripture says: Man does not live on bread alone but on every word that comes from the mouth of God.'

Mt 4:1-4

For personal reflection

What desires/temptations do I routinely give in to?

How can I journey more closely to God?

of what they have done, that they have broken their covenant with God, and have betrayed the truth of who they are themselves.

In the gospel, we see Jesus in the desert fasting and confronting temptation. The images are very powerful and again quite stark. Here, the tempter still seeks to deceive, to convince Jesus that something that is wrong is actually good. There is no doubt that what he offers is desirable. This is one thing that these two stories have in common – what is not good for us is presented as desirable. We know this to be true. Forbidden fruit is always sweeter. We don't want anything that's bad for us until we're told we can't have it. For us, it's not always the thing itself that we're struggling with, but rather the actual desire. Are we masters of our lives, our bodies, or are we subject to our desires? Are we able to sort out those desires which are good for us from those which are not, especially when the desires themselves work to convince us that all desire is good? And our desires are quite different to our needs. I'm in awe of those who truly master their desire, because it is an area where most of us struggle, whether it is the desire for power, for foods, for drink, for sex, for drugs, whatever. Those who suffer addictions know what it is to be a slave of desire.

The three hallmarks of Lent for Christians, prayer, fasting and almsgiving, are recognised in our tradition as things that help to break the power of our desires. They help to recognise the truth of who we are, who we are called to be; they help us to hear the voice of God's Spirit as he prompts us in the ways of truth and goodness. They are aids to lead us into the freedom we long for as children of God. It is in freedom that we are called to live as God's children, and the greatest enslavers are not the external things of the world, but what is inside. We have just set out on Ash Wednesday on this Lenten journey; it's meant to be something of a desert journey, a time where we face the temptations of life. The goal is Easter, the goal is the renewal of our lives as followers of Christ, fit to celebrate the resurrection of Christ as his faithful disciples.

---

[37] Genesis 2:7-9.3:1-7
    Psalm 50:3-6.12-14.17 R.V.3
    Romans 5:12-19
    Matthew 4:1-11
[38] Homily given on 13 March 2011
[39] (Sermon 6 on Lent, 1-2, from the Office of Readings for the
    Thursday after Ash Wednesday)

SECOND SUNDAY OF LENT[4041]
GOOD TO BE HERE

A few years ago in Italy I went mountain climbing or hill walking, with two extremely fit, enthusiastic and experienced men. It was a high enough mountain, at least to my Irish eyes; there was snow on the top! The other two were gung-ho, and again and again, they left me standing trying to get my breath. They were really eager to get as near to the top as possible. I don't know if you've ever had the experience of climbing a hill in the company of an enthusiast; some of them are inclined to set off at a great old pace, and you're one of the stragglers at the back. I imagine that when Jesus and his four disciples were on the way up Mount Tabor, that Jesus was way out ahead of the others. I imagine him climbing this holy mountain, knowing it to be the place of his encounter with the Father. I imagine his enthusiasm to get there, and the disciples following behind, struggling to catch their breath, their muscles aching. Maybe they were saying that it was a good idea when they were at the bottom, but halfway up, not so sure. Climbing Croagh Patrick is pretty much the same – a great idea when you're at the bottom, the worst idea you've ever had when you're halfway up, and pretty good when you eventually reach the top and you're lucky enough to see the magnificent view. But when the disciples eventually arrived at the top of the mountain and witnessed the transfiguration of Jesus, they were dazzled and amazed, and had no desire to leave. "Let us make three tents," Peter says. He wants to stay. And who wouldn't want to stay? But we have to come down from all the heights we experience; we have to descend from all the mountains we climb.

Jesus took with him Peter and James and his brother John and led them up a high mountain where they could be alone. There in their presence he was transfigured; his face shone like the sun and his clothes became as white as the light. Suddenly Moses and Elijah appeared to them; they were talking with him. Then Peter spoke to Jesus. 'Lord,' he said 'it is wonderful for us to be here; if you wish, I will make three tents here, one for you, one for Moses and one for Elijah.' He was still speaking when suddenly a bright cloud covered them with shadow, and from the crowd there came a voice which said, 'This is my Son, the Beloved; he enjoys my favour. Listen to him'

Mt 17:1-5

FOR PERSONAL REFLECTION

How does the image of the transfigured Christ sustain me in my Lenten faith journey?

As we follow Christ, we are sometimes blessed with times of great joy and love, times of insight and understanding, and we want to stay there. These are the times when it all makes sense, when we feel close to God, and experience a sense of his presence that we never want to let go of. They're the times when we're like Peter, we want to remain there. We want the good times to last. We want our faith experience always to be uplifting, dazzling even. But we can't stay there. Quite a lot of the time, our faith journey is uphill, like climbing a mountain. Sometimes it's a struggle; sometimes it's boring, mundane. We wonder where God is, what it's all about, does he listen to our prayers?

The other great image of scripture is the journey in the desert, a place of aridity, dryness. So much of our faith journey is spent in the desert, broken by moments of extraordinary insight and joy from time to time. The desert times, or the times when we are climbing the mountain, these are the times of growth and development.

In our first reading we hear of the story of Abraham who began as Abram and was asked by God to leave his own people and his own land for a land that the Lord would give him. All through his life Abraham was guided by the promise of God, often with little evidence that the promise would be fulfilled. Yet he was faithful. Abraham is called our father in faith. We are called to imitate his example by following the Transfigured Lord and putting our trust in him. The disciples had the wonderful experience of witnessing the transfiguration, seeing Jesus in his glory. It was an experience that they must have pondered on and considered, wondering what it meant, an experience that gave them encouragement and new heart in times when the Master they were following seemed difficult to understand. In the days to come, the disciples would face the suffering and death of Jesus, and afterwards they would face suffering themselves. The experience of the transfiguration when Jesus was revealed as the Son of God was given to them to sustain them in those very days, to let them see the truth of the One they followed.

For us the image of the transfigured body of Christ is an image also of what lies ahead for us – the image of the transfigured Body of Christ. We gather today as the body of Christ, and we look forward to the time when we as that one Body are transfigured in him, and the glory of God's children is revealed.

For some, Lent may well be a joyless time, a time for doing without and not too many highs. But for us who believe, joy should characterise our Lent, because this season is about renewal, turning to God again as we prepare for the celebration of Easter and all that that means. This is the time to do a bit of spade work in our faith, the time to deepen our relationship with God, to tackle the obstacles to faith in our lives, to discipline ourselves as disciples as we follow our Risen Lord on this journey of faith. And it's not too late to start. May the experience of the transfiguration be for us an encouragement in these Lenten days, sustaining us on our spiritual journey.

---

[40] Genesis 12:1-4
Psalm 32:4-5.18-20.22 R.V 22
2 Timothy 1:8-10
Matthew 17:1-9
[41] Homily given on 17 February 2008

Third Sunday of Lent[4243]
Living water

Lent is often described as a desert space, a place of dryness and barrenness, a place where we experience a certain deprivation. The forty years spent in the desert by the people of Israel as they journeyed from slavery in Egypt to the Promised Land of Canaan, and the forty days of fasting which Jesus undertook as he began his ministry both form part of the background of this season. As communities we are asked to re-engage with our thirst, to ask ourselves "what is it we thirst for?" We're asked to discover again our need of God, our thirst for his presence, for his life. But to do so without also engaging with the physical hunger and thirst of people throughout the world is wrong. Our spiritual journey in Lent is made visible in the outward journey of care and concern for others. The traditional works of prayer and fasting support the all-important almsgiving, the care of others. Our faith is in Jesus, the Word made flesh, the physical expression of God's presence. And so our spiritual path is reflected in our engagement with the physical world, with society and with the needs of all God's people.

The gospel story today tells of the gripping encounter between Jesus and a Samaritan woman, a woman who was despised even in her own community. As a Samaritan and as a sinner, this woman was on the margins, not someone with whom a respectable Jewish rabbi would converse. And yet here is Jesus, engaging her in this strange conversation about water. Pretty soon you realise that he's not talking about water from the well, physical water that you drink. His thirst is deeper, and he knows that she thirsts. Jesus thirsts for those who do not know the way, for those who are lost in life, for sinners; he

Jesus came to the Samaritan town called Sychar and tired by the journey, sat straight down by the well. It was about the sixth hour. When a Samaritan woman came to draw water, Jesus said to her, 'Give me a drink.' His disciples had gone into the town to buy food. The Samaritan woman said to him, 'What? You are a Jew and you ask me, a Samaritan, for a drink?' - Jews, in fact, do not associate with Samaritans. Jesus replied: 'If you only knew what God is offering and who it is that is saying to you: Give me a drink, you would have been the one to ask, and he would have given you living water.'

Jn 4:5-10

For personal reflection

In this season of Lent, where in my life am I thirsting for God?

thirsts for their faith. The woman has a thirst she does not recognise, the thirst for life, the thirst for truth, the thirst for God. She stands for us. And it is Jesus who promises to quench her thirst.

Here midway through Lent, he promises to quench our thirst too. In Lent, we experience thirst; at Easter that living water is released.

Throughout this season this water is welling up; it seems that it's building up in pressure. It will flow from the side and heart of Christ on the cross on Good Friday; it will be poured on those who are baptised at Easter, and at Pentecost, there will be a tremendous outpouring of the Spirit into the hearts and lives of ordinary people at Pentecost, because this living water is the gift of the Spirit. This time from Lent to Pentecost is one seamless act of renewal. The living water promised today bursts through at Easter, and is given in abundance at Pentecost. The gift of living water has already been given to us, at baptism and again at Confirmation. It remains within us, a little spring, which we may not even be aware of, but which has the potential to change our lives utterly if we choose to quench our thirst at this source.

There are so many unhappy people in our society, so many people searching, like the woman of Samaria. There are many like her, whose self-worth and self-esteem are poor, people who experience rejection, people who seem to have little purpose in life. To all of them and to all of us, Jesus says, "I know your thirst, and I thirst for you; I thirst for your love and for your faith. And I offer you living water. Come, drink and be satisfied."

---

[42] Exodus 17:3-7
   Psalm 94:1-2.6-9.R V.8
   Romans 5:1-2,5-8
   John 4:5-42
[43] Homily given on 23 February 2008

FOURTH SUNDAY OF LENT[4445]
BLIND TO THE LIGHT

There's a gentleman from the Congo preparing for baptism in Carlow at present. His name is Moses, and during the week he was presented with the Creed at one of the Masses in the Cathedral. The Creed is the statement of our beliefs, the key to our faith; and the congregation recited the Creed to Moses, who listened and received. It was a symbolic action of handing on our faith and belief.

One of the articles of the Creed refers to our belief in the communion of saints. This is the community of all those who live in God's presence, the saints we pray to and the saints who are forgotten. For the members of the early Church, the communion of saints referred to the entire Christian community. If you were baptised, you were one of the saints, a man or woman who now lived in the light of God, a person who had left the darkness of sin and was now a child of God, living as Christ lived. St Paul often refers to the communities he writes to as saints "you are God's saints" he says. And I wonder, do we see ourselves as saints? There's almost a presumption in the scriptures that we should be, but somehow, I think we're embarrassed. We have notions that saints are somehow different than we are. People have certainly lost a sense of sin or of being sinners, I don't know that now we see ourselves as saints either. "I'm no holy Joe," "I'm spiritual but not religious", as if you could be one without the other, "I have my own beliefs", but they're not shared with anyone.

During Lent some of the great symbols of faith are put before us. Last week, it was water, our thirst for living water, our need of baptism in Christ, to live in the living water of his Spirit. This week,

As Jesus went along, he saw a man who had been blind from birth. He spat on the ground, made a paste with the spittle, put this over the eyes of the blind man and said to him, 'God and wash in the Pool of Siloam' (a name that means 'sent'). So the blind man went off and washed himself, and came away with his sight restored.

His neighbours who earlier had seen him begging said, 'Isn't this the man who used to sit and beg?' Some said, 'Yes, it is the same one.' Others said, 'No, he only looks like him.' The man himself said, 'I am the man.'

Jn 9:1-9

FOR PERSONAL REFLECTION

Am I the person God created me to be?

Am I living the life that God wants me to live? If not, what do I need to change about my life?

the symbol is light. The story of the blind man is presented. It's quite a long and involved story; we have just heard a part of it. There's a lot of tension in it. Jesus heals the physical blindness of the man and sends him to wash in the waters of the Pool of Siloam – reminder of the waters of baptism. For the Jews of the time, physical blindness was a sign that the man was a sinner. Any grave illness was regarded as a punishment. Jesus set out to correct that way of thinking. His encounters with the blind man are accompanied by a call to leave the darkness and to believe in the light. Jesus is the light. He is the one who heals the darkness of sin. Jesus highlights the contrast between the Pharisees whose physical sight was perfect, and the blind man. They do not recognise the light. Their eyes of faith are blind; they do not see the light. They do not recognise Christ. The blind man sees him immediately and recognises him for who he is, and, we are told, he worships him.

I think that sometimes we're like the Pharisees; we have no serious wrongdoing in our lives, no darkness that we're aware of, but no light either. Our hearts are not on fire. We're blind and we do not know it. We do not see Christ or hear his voice in any significant way, in any way that changes the way we live. When we were baptised, our parents and godparents lit a candle for us from the Easter candle, the sign of Christ's life and light. They were entrusted with the light of faith, and they handed it on to us. We were called children of the light in our baptism; we were called to see the light, to stand in the light, to walk in the light and to be the light – as St. Paul says at the start of the second reading "You were darkness once, but now you are light in the Lord."

This language of light and darkness is very symbolic - but does it touch us? Is it real for us? If we want to discover whether or not we're walking in light, the question we might ask is "am I happy?" Am I the person God created me to be? Am I living the life that God wants me to live? Or am I wandering about in the dark, looking for light?

---

[44] 1 Samuel 16:1. 6-7. 10-13
    Psalm 22 R V. 1
    Ephesians 5:8-14
    John 9:1-41
[45] Homily given on 2 March 2008

FIFTH SUNDAY OF LENT[4647]
LIFE AFTER DEATH

The gospels are full of great stories, and this one has it all – tragedy and sadness, suspense and tension, building up to a climax of deliverance and liberation. We tell this story as we come closer to Easter; at one level it acts as a precursor for what is to come, the death and resurrection of Jesus, but at another level, it simply points to the inadequacy of our hopes for this life, which are surpassed by far in the resurrection. The return of Lazarus to life was not of the same order as the resurrection of Jesus. Lazarus simply returned to the life which he had left; after being raised from the dead, life for him was no different than before, and death still lay ahead. On the other hand, the resurrection of Jesus is an altogether different phenomenon – something completely new. Jesus rose to a life that has no end, a life where death has no more power and exists no more. Although his body rose from the tomb, it was utterly transformed, so much so that the disciples and witnesses to the resurrection had difficulty recognising him at first. Today Jesus shows that he is master even of death, that he can call forth Lazarus from the tomb, but what lies ahead is very different, for in his resurrection from the dead, he opens up a new possibility for humanity, a transformed life which has no end.

We tend to be a bit vague about what happens to people after death. We pray that they go to heaven; by that we mean that they will be in a place of happiness with God, with all the saints and angels, and be united once more with all the loved ones and friends who have died. In our tradition we pray for the dead; not all the Christian Churches do this. The scriptural basis for our practice is in the Book of the Maccabees, where prayers are offered for those who have died after having turned to false gods. We pray for our dead because we are realistic enough to know that many people die

When Martha heard that Jesus had come she went to meet him. Mary remained sitting in the house. Martha said to Jesus, 'If you had been here, my brother would not have died, but I know that even now, whatever you ask of God, he will grant you,' 'your brother' said Jesus to her 'will rise again.' Martha said, 'I know he will rise again at the resurrection on the last day.' Jesus said:

'I am the resurrection and the life. If anyone believes in me, even though he dies he will live. And whoever lives and believes in me will never die. Do you believe this?'

'Yes Lord,' she said 'I believe that you are the Christ, the Son of God, the one who was to come into this world.'

Jn 11:20-27

FOR PERSONAL REFLECTION

What do I need to be freed from in my life?

What is preventing me from living as God wants?

without having lived the best of lives, and before they enter the presence of God, who is all light and goodness, the darkness within them is cleansed. We call that state of preparation for heaven, Purgatory. A lot of people tend to dismiss belief in Purgatory; others see it as a place to be feared, a place of punishment. But I think that in fact our belief in Purgatory is something very positive, something optimistic. It means that there is hope of redemption for all, even those who have sinned grievously. Otherwise, how could God respect their freedom and yet welcome them home to him? Essentially Purgatory is a state of preparation for those who have not yet entered heaven, and we believe that our prayers help those who have died and progress that preparation, whatever form it may take.

Hell is another state that we tend to be vague about. We don't know what form it may have, and there are many who would reject its existence altogether. But God respects our free will, and if someone can definitively reject God, and by that I mean reject all that is good, or life-giving, or in any way loving, then God respects that choice, and will allow them to be in a state where he is totally absent. That possibility exists, but is there anyone so capable of rejecting all that is good? Who knows? The Church has often named people whom it believes to be in heaven, but it has never said that anyone was in hell.

We also believe in the resurrection of the body; this is part of the Creed, the statement of faith that is common to all the Christian Churches. We believe that we will be raised from the dead, body and soul, and that this new transformed life that Jesus won in the resurrection will be ours. But that won't come until the end of time, and the last day. In the meantime, those who die are in heaven. When the resurrection comes, body, soul and spirit, will be one in the fullness of life in heaven with God. The resurrection of Jesus together with his ascension, points to this.

And so today, we look forward as we witness the power of Jesus over death and anticipate his resurrection to new life. And in the words of the gospel, we ask him "to unbind us," to free us from all that imprisons us and prevents us from living as God wants. We ask him to unbind us so that we might live in the freedom of God's children, freedom from all sin and temptation, freedom to love and live in peace.

---

[46] Ezekiel 37:12-12
   Psalm 129: R. v 7
   Romans 8:8-11
   John 11:1-45
[47] Homily given on 10 April 2011

Easter Vigil[4849]
Darkness to light

We came into the Cathedral this evening in darkness; we had to find our way, and carefully walk and not bump into things or fall over. One light alone illuminated the gloom. One light alone led us from the yard outside where the fire had been blessed in the obscurity of night. One light alone was shared among us, so that the lights held by each one of us here were a flame of that one light, which alone was held high above, leading us forward, guiding us into the darkness of the church. That light was the light of the Paschal Candle – the Easter Candle, the light of Christ.

In these days of Holy Week, we have followed Christ as he entered into the darkness of human suffering and anguish. We have united our darkness with his – the crosses we carry are his, the sufferings we bear are his. "Ecce Homo" declared Pontius Pilate on Good Friday, as he presented the scourged Christ crowned with thorns to the people "Behold the man." This is what we do to Sons of God, behold the man. In him is the story of all humanity. This is what humanity does to humanity. Behold Christ and his suffering and see how he suffered in his people throughout the world, in every war-torn country, in every place where people are diminished, in every person who has born pain or anxiety, physical, mental or spiritual suffering. Behold Christ and see yourself.

We followed Christ to Calvary, and he led us from there to his tomb, where the Church has been waiting in silence, watching. Now in the darkness of this night, the light has come. Jesus is Risen – Alleluia is our song. Jesus is Risen, and with

Come and see the place where he lay, then go quickly and tell his disciples, "He has risen from the dead and now he is going before you to Galilee; it is there you will see him." Now I have told you.' Filled with awe and great joy the women came quickly away from the tomb and ran to tell the disciples.

Mt 28:6-7

FOR PERSONAL REFLECTION

Celebrate this new day, the day of Christ.

65

him, humanity is raised up. Jesus has journeyed into the darkness of the tomb, into the very womb of Death; he has journeyed into the darkness of hopelessness and despair, that place where life is absent, where hope does not exist. And in that place, he is light; he is hope; he is new life. For all lost in the dark, for all who stumble and cannot find their way, for those trapped in addictions, for those alienated from society, for those alienated even from themselves – he says, "Come, I give you life – a new life, a life without end, a life totally different to anything you can ever have imagined. Come to this life, where there is no more death, no more darkness, not the life you have before, but something utterly other, utterly new and changed." Today we celebrate a new day, the day of Christ, a day without end, for the darkness has been conquered and death deprived of all power. This is truly the dawn of a new Creation.

Near 1600 years ago in 433, St. Patrick lit the Easter fire in the darkness of the Hill of Slane; it was a challenge to the culture of the druids, wise men of society, who said that the fire lit that night would never be extinguished in Ireland. That one light alone has been burning in this country ever since. We are here, taking part in this celebration tonight, because that one light has been lit in us and for us.

[48] Genesis 1:1-2:2   Psalm 103(104):1-2,5-6,10,12-14,24,35
Genesis 22:1-18   Psalm 15(16):5,8-11
Exodus 14:15-15:1   Exodus 15
Isaiah 54:5-14   Psalm 29(30):2,4-6,11-13
Isaiah 55:1-11   Isaiah 12
Baruch 3:9-15,32-4:4   Psalm 18(19):8-11
Ezekiel 36:16-17,18-28   Psalm 41(42):2-3,5,42:3-4
Romans 6:3-11   Psalm 117(118):1-2, 16-17, 22-23
Matthew 28:1-10
[49] Homily given on 23 April 2011

Easter Sunday[5051]
An empty tomb

Holy Saturday is a very special day in the year. It's a day of rest, recalling the seventh day after creation when the Lord rested. But on Holy Saturday, it is in the tomb that Christ rests in the sleep of death. There's a stillness on Holy Saturday, as if the world is waiting; there's a void, a sense of absence in the air. Where is Christ? The horror of the arrest of Jesus on Holy Thursday night, his trial and torture on Good Friday, culminating in his brutal execution on the Cross - all have taken their toll, and now there is silence. For the disciples, it was the silence of fear, the silence of betrayal, of having abandoned him, the silent trauma of losing one so filled with love and grace, having him taken from them so suddenly and so violently. And now, nothing, only shame. Now all of that horror is past; Saturday was a day of calm after the storm of cruelty. But not only was the terror over, but so too their dreams were gone, their hopes for the future. Everything the twelve apostles had looked forward to, believed in - all gone; they were stranded, lost, afraid. The other disciples had lost Jesus but probably also lost faith in the twelve, the group closest to Jesus; one had betrayed Christ, another denied him, most of the others abandoned him. They were leaderless, scattered, without direction.

Is it like that for many Catholics in Ireland today? Is the Irish experience a Holy Saturday experience? After the horror of the abuse scandals, some of which still continue to be revealed, are we in a Holy Saturday space? - lost, leaderless, not having confidence in the successors of the apostles, and no sign of Jesus. The affluence of the Tiger years followed by recession and the new dependency

Then the other disciple who had reached the tomb first also went in; he saw and believed. Till this moment they had failed to understand the teaching of scripture, that he must rise from the dead.

Jn 20:8-9

For personal reflection

Walk in the light of faith.

on technology has changed us. Not just that, but our society has changed so much and so fast, that we hardly know who we are or where we're going. Everything we believed in and hoped for, now open to question, as all our certainties have been shaken. I wonder.

But today is Easter Sunday - it's the Day of Resurrection, the day of light, the day of joy, the day of New Life rising from the stillness of the tomb. Death, in all its terror and darkness, is conquered; sin is vanquished. This is a day of hope.

And on this day, the women went early to the tomb, before dawn; they went in the darkness. That's a significant detail; the light had not arrived, the dawn had not yet come. There are so many today who walk in darkness. They went with heavy hearts, to do their duties for the dead and anoint the body. But it was not there, and they came away in fear, rushing to tell the apostles. And Peter and John came running to the tomb, John, the disciple Jesus loved, running faster. And they found an empty tomb.

Like them we are asked to put our faith in an empty tomb. He is not here; he is risen. There is no body. So often in our faith, it is not by signs of his presence that God is revealed, but rather by signs of his absence. It is in the intangible, in the things we struggle to grasp, in the things beyond us, that God reveals himself. We can't put our finger on it; we can't prove it, but we know he's there; we know he loves us; we trust and we have faith. And it's all the harder to have faith when trust has been broken; yet Peter, who denied Christ and abandoned him, is still called to be his first witness, not John who was there at the end on Calvary. It is Peter, the one who denied Jesus and abandoned him who is the rock and who is first to enter the tomb.

For Christians, faith always involves a risk, and we are asked again and again to take one more step in faith. The empty tomb points to the God whose presence is revealed in absence; the God whose presence is Absence - seeing his Risen Body will come later. Today is about faith or it's about nothing. And in that faith, we discover the life that lies hidden within, the life of the risen Christ, living in us. As St Paul puts it, "you have died, and now the life you have is hidden with Christ in God. But when Christ is revealed - and he is our life - you too will be revealed in all your glory with him." Yes, we have died with Christ, but now we are called to rise with him, to share his life, to recognise him with joyful hearts in trust and confidence and hope.

Like the women, we must journey often in the darkness, but today we are invited to come into the light of the new day of Christ, the light of faith, the day which offers meaning to those for whom life has lost its meaning; the day that offers hope to those who have none; the day that offers Christ to a people who look for new life. This is the day of the Lord: rejoice, for we are an Easter People.

[50] Acts 10:34, 37-43
    Psalm 114:1-2, 16-17, 22-23
    Colossians 3:1-4
    John 20:1-9
[51] Homily given on 20 April 2014

Today Pope Benedict will beatify the late Pope John Paul II; it's the first step on the way to canonisation, and it recognises his personal holiness and closeness to God. Beatification is about the recognition that this was a holy person, a man to whom the Christians can pray, asking his intercession and guidance; it's not about his politics, his administration or anything else. Pope John Paul was both a very popular and controversial leader but included in the legacy he has left the Church is the devotion to the Divine Mercy. This devotion to Christ as Divine Mercy originated from the visions of St. Faustina Kowalska in Poland in the last century, and the feast of the Divine Mercy was instituted by Pope John Paul on the second Sunday of Easter, also known as Low Sunday, in other words, it's today.

Now whether or not you're committed to the particular devotion of the Divine Mercy is a matter for the individual spirituality of each person. Our religion recognises many different devotions, including the devotion to the Sacred Heart of Jesus, the Immaculate Heart of Mary, devotion to Our Lady under various titles, Our Lady of Lourdes, Our Lady of Knock, Our Lady of Fatima, of Guadalupe and so on. All of these enshrine particular insights about the Christian message or highlight different characteristics of Jesus or Our Lady, which can help us to grow in faith and holiness. Whether or not we adopt the devotion itself is a matter of choice for individuals, but the insight of the devotion is something that is true for all of us and for our faith. The feast of Divine Mercy, and the devotion to the Divine Mercy, point towards the infinite mercy of

Then he said to Thomas, "Put your finger here; see my hands. Reach out your hand and put it into my side. Stop doubting and believe."

Thomas said to him, "My Lord and my God!"

Then Jesus told him, "Because you have seen me, you have believed; blessed are those who have not seen and yet have believed."

Jn 20:27-31

FOR PERSONAL REFLECTION

Be merciful!

our God, and to the invitation that is given to all people at all times and places, to come and to experience that mercy, to share it with others, and to grow in that love. The devotion to Divine Mercy is a new expression of something that has been around since Christ himself walked the earth, and it has many other expressions. The charism of the Mercy Sisters, for example, is a particular expression of Divine Mercy, but offered in a very different form and context.

The prayers of today's Mass reflect the mercy of God, because the gospel of today places mercy and forgiveness right at the heart of the Christian message. We see Jesus appearing to his disciples for the first time since his death. This is the evening of the day of resurrection, the evening of the first Easter Sunday, the first day of the week, the evening of that day when the women went to the tomb early in the morning, found it empty, and received the message from the angel. Now Jesus appears among his followers in spite of the locked doors in the upper room, and his first words are "Peace be with you." Those words are very significant, because they describe the relationship that must exist among the followers of Jesus – we are to be at peace with one another, to extend the hand of friendship to one another, to respect the just rights of others, to alleviate their needs. Peace is about the harmony that exists under God, when all are respected and thrive. And that is the vision of Christian life. Next Jesus gives the gift of his Spirit to his followers. This is a recognition that the power of God among us is necessary to live the peace that Jesus asks; the peace that he gives is not the peace that the world knows, the simple absence of war and hostility, but the peace that comes from living in union with our God, and so with one another. Following from this is the call for forgiveness, the call to let go of the hurts and resentments that prevent us from living in peace with others. We are called to forgive and to extend to others the mercy that comes from God. Jesus himself gave this example when, while he was hanging on the cross, he called on his Father to forgive his persecutors and executioners. This forgiveness was given without any apology or expression of regret; it came even while Christ was still suffering, and his tormenters were still venting their hatred and tormenting him. This is the standard of forgiveness that we, as followers of Christ, are called to extend to others; it is also the standard of mercy that our God offers to us: unconditional loving mercy.

Our society needs mercy; it needs people to proclaim and live a message of peace for all, a peace that is rooted in God's love and nourished by his mercy. Our society needs that peace, not because people have done wrong and now ask for forgiveness and mercy, but rather because people have been hurt and carry that hurt like a heavy weight, a hurt that prevents them from living as fully as they could. We are asked to forgive others for our own sakes, so that we can live at peace, not for the sake of those who have wronged us. Thomas was not with the disciples when Jesus appeared. We're told that he refused to believe unless he could see the evidence of Jesus' death, the wounds. We're not told that he couldn't believe; we're told rather that he refused to believe, which is a bit different. It's as if the hurt and the pain and the grief of Jesus' death, the guilt and sorrow for having run away and abandoned him: all these are burdens too heavy to bear, burdens that prevent him moving on. It is only when he sees the Lord and receives his peace himself, that he can let go and give his heart to the Lord in his act of faith "My Lord and my God."

I'm sure that devotion to the Divine Mercy gave Pope John Paul the courage and generosity to reach out in forgiveness to the man who shot him in 1981. We pray that the mercy of God may be experienced by all of us and by all Christians, so that we may witness to his message of peace through the power of the Holy Spirit.

Jesus offers his peace and his mercy in the Eucharist and in the sacrament of reconciliation. As we come here today, may we welcome these gifts, and allow them to grow within us, so that the mercy of God may free us from our burdens and enable us to live in peace with ourselves, with others and with our God.

[52] Acts 2:42-47
Psalm 117:2-4, 22-24
I Peter 1:3-9
John 20:19-31
[53] Homily given on 1 May 2011

The story of the encounter of the two disciples with Jesus on the road to Emmaus appeals to our imagination. There's so much we don't know: why didn't they recognise him? Why were they leaving the city so soon? Were they leaving in fear? Where did they stay in Emmaus, and what was the point of their journey? And who were they: we're only given the name of one of them, Cleopas. This appearance occurred on the evening of that first Easter day, when Christ rose from the dead, but these two aren't hanging around to find out what it was all about; instead they were leaving behind the fear and horror of Jesus' death, but are not yet ready for the revelation of his rising from the grave.

Jesus often walks with us unknown and unrecognised. If we were to reflect on the times when our hearts burned within us, when we were given strength or were sustained in some way, then we might come to realise that here may be found the presence of Jesus, who never abandons his people, but walks with us, even in the times of fear or horror that we might face. Every Christian makes that journey to Emmaus at some stage in their lives; we may make it several times. It's the journey from desperation into hope; the journey from death to new life; the journey from sin to forgiveness. We make that journey in the company of others, but most especially in the company of the one who transforms our experiences of hurt with his love. His beatitudes remind us of the blessedness that lies in finding him in our suffering, in not losing hope in the times when life challenges us.

When he was at the table with them, he took bread, gave thanks, broke it and began to give it to them. Then their eyes were opened and they recognized him, and he disappeared from their sight. They asked each other, "Were not our hearts burning within us while he talked with us on the road and opened the Scriptures to us?"

Lk 24:30-32

FOR PERSONAL REFLECTION

Open your hearts to receive Jesus, to welcome Him and to recognize Him!

The story is shaped to resemble the structure of the Mass, so that just as at the beginning of Mass, we acknowledge our sinfulness, the poverty of our humanity, so too the disciples acknowledge and leave behind the hurt and disappointments, the betrayal and denial of the events in Jerusalem. Jesus then uses the scripture to explain to them who he is and what his dying was about, just as we listen to the Word of God and hear it broken for us and applied to life. Jesus then takes his place at table with the disciples, and we see the ritual that was part of many meals Jesus shared with his followers, but which took on a new significance at the Last Supper, when he took the bread and blessed it, broke it and gave it to them. This was the moment when they recognised him. The liturgy of the Eucharist repeats those actions, and like the disciples, we too are invited to recognise him in the breaking of bread. And so it is that full of joy and hope, nourished by his presence in Word and Sacrament, we are sent out at the end of Mass to share the Good News with others; so it was that the disciples returned to Jerusalem, eager to tell of their experience of the Resurrection of Jesus.

This story was used in the early Church to encourage those disciples who may have been disappointed that Jesus had not returned after his Ascension. It reminded them, just as it reminds us, that Jesus is with us, that we meet him in Word and Sacrament in the Eucharist. It invites us to open our hearts to receive him, to welcome him, to recognise him. The resurrection is not about something that happened 2000 years ago; it's about the presence of Jesus with us now, the same Jesus who strengthens and encourages us, just as he did his disciples on the road to Emmaus.

---

[54] Acts 2:14, 22-33
  Psalm 15:1-2, 7-11
  1 Peter 1:17-21
  Luke 24:13-35
[55] Homily given on 4 May 2014

Fourth Sunday of Easter[5657]
A full life

Today is not just Vocations Sunday, the fourth Sunday of Easter, it also marks the beginning of a year of vocation, a year in which the Irish Church focuses especially on the call of Christ to each one. It's the Year of Vocation, not vocations, as it recognises that the first and most significant call for each one of us is the call of our baptism – the call to follow Christ. How we follow him, whether as single people, married people, religious or priests, or how we choose to serve him in the community, all of that comes after that first and primary call of our baptism. We have been graced by God as his people, born again in baptism as his sons and daughters. And so we are asked this year to reflect on the call of our baptism, how we are each called to follow Christ, how we are to live our faith, how is Christ asking us to serve, how are we called to live as Jesus lives, how are we called to witness to his gospel in the concrete situations of our families, our jobs, our community?

One of the striking things about society is the extent to which people are dissatisfied with one aspect or other of their lives. In 1986, 75% of people were satisfied with their job; in 2006 only 34% said they were happy with their job. A survey taken in the spring of 2007 asked people what their New Year Resolution was, and 42% of those surveyed said that their New Resolution was to get a new job. It makes you wonder about the cause of all of this – is it the increased affluence of our society? Is it the increasing secularisation? I believe that we cannot achieve real fulfilment unless we embrace God's plan for us; we cannot achieve real happiness unless we welcome and follow our vocation – the call that God gives us to serve him in a particular way. I wonder how many

Therefore Jesus said again, "Very truly I tell you, I am the gate for the sheep. All who have come before me are thieves and robbers, but the sheep have not listened to them. I am the gate; whoever enters through me will be saved. They will come in and go out, and find pasture. The thief comes only to steal and kill and destroy; I have come that they may have life, and have it to the full.

Jn 10:7-10

For personal reflection

Follow Christ;
walk in His ways.

75

people pray about making the right choices in life – certainly their parents pray for them. But unless we are where God wants us to be, something is missing.

All of this dissatisfaction comes against the backdrop of decreasing vocations to the priesthood and religious life. I'm not saying that's the answer either. But I do think that the changing face of the Irish Church in itself represents a call to respond in a new way to the gospel. Even if there were a major upturn in the numbers entering seminaries and novitiates, the call for all Christians to reflect anew on their role in the Church is an urgent one. We are at a stage where the need for lay people to take responsibility for their local Church is pressing. Within our diocese, so much of the vital work of evangelisation is being done by lay people; yet there is much more to be done at so many different levels from catechesis, youth work, care for the sick and housebound, management, care for relationships and marriages, the bereaved, the newcomers and so on. This Year of Vocation is an opportunity for us to cultivate a culture of vocation in our diocese and in our parish, so that we can respond as Church to the call of the gospel.

Today Christ tells us that he has come that we may have life in its fullness; only through him can we enter the fullness of life; only in him will we find the fulfilment and happiness that our hearts desire, only in listening to his voice and doing his will. He is the door; he is the way. As each of us discerns our way in life, let us come to him; let us listen to his voice; let us ask ourselves and let us ask him how we are to serve him in today's world. Let us create a climate of vocation, a place where we as a Church and as individuals listen to the voice of our Shepherd.

---

[56] Acts 2:14, 36-41
Psalm 22:1-6
1 Peter 2:20-25
John 10:1-10
[57] Homily given on 13 April 2008

People often wonder why Jesus isn't still around, why he had to ascend to the Father after the Resurrection, why he doesn't make regular appearances and show his glory so that no one would ever have any doubts about the Christian message and way of life. Why do we have to live by faith, not by certainty? We have a lot of questions but not all the answers. What we do know is that Jesus returned to the Father to complete his mission, which was to open heaven to human beings, to restore us to life again, to conquer sin and death, and to bring us into the life of God. In his return to the Father, a human being, Jesus Christ, God in human flesh, has entered heaven, thus opening the way for all humans to enter the new life of heaven, in body as well as soul. But Jesus didn't leave us alone; he sent the Holy Spirit among his followers to guide them, to enlighten them, to console them, and to lead them to life with God. The Spirit of God is given to complete his work on earth, to lead us into this new life.

In the gospel today, we hear Jesus preparing his followers for the coming of the Spirit; the words are quite mystical as they describe the union of Jesus with the Father and the Spirit, and the invitation that is ours to be part of that union. We are told that the Spirit is with us; the Spirit is in us. He tells us that he is in the Father, that we are in him, and he in us. We have very little idea of what that means. We know that we are called to share in the divine life, to share in the life of God. Part of it is about how we live, the good things we do, the care we show to others, our honesty and integrity and so on; but it's also about actually being in relationship with our God, having a true relationship. The life of God is present in us now, although we may not be aware of it; it's not just something we will find at

Jesus answered: "Don't you know me, Philip, even after I have been among you such a long time? Anyone who has seen me has seen the Father. How can you say, 'Show us the Father'?

Jn 14:9

FOR PERSONAL REFLECTION

Always have an answer ready for people who ask you the reason for the hope that you have.

the end. Our task is to nourish this relationship, to grow in our appreciation of the presence of God among us, to live more fully and more deeply the life of the Spirit that has been given to us. In fact we are called to be mystics, to live the divine life, not just in the life to come, but to live it now, to grow in our union with God in the circumstances of our everyday life.

Every now and then I notice how we struggle with the whole notion of growing in our faith or struggle even to understand that growing in faith is part of being a Christian. We seem to come to a stage in our relationship with God where we're happy enough; we don't want to be disturbed in it; we don't want to be taken for a holy Joe. But if we don't grow in our faith, there's a danger that it will stagnate, a danger that when it is tested, it won't be strong enough to withstand the trials. Nothing in life stays the same; the Spirit is given to us to help us grow in our life as Christians, to lead us in an ever-deeper relationship with God.

St. Peter reminds us in the second reading that we should always have an answer ready for people who ask us the reason for the hope that we all have. That means knowing our faith, knowing and understanding what it means, what it's about, what it teaches. It's particularly relevant for those who have children, particularly children who question, who want answers, who want to understand or simply to see can they catch you out. But it's important for everyone. In the past, the many religious magazines that you'd find in Catholic homes gave some support to us by providing more information about issues of faith or prayer or whatever. Many of them are still available. But we also have the help of the internet, the many resources that the diocese makes available, as well as religious books, DVDs etc. There's plenty of help. But nothing can help us as much as the Spirit of God, who gives the gifts of wisdom and understanding. It is in our relationship with the Spirit of truth that we come to discern the truth of God's love and the life that he calls us to live.

---

[58] Acts 6:1-7
  Psalm 32:1-2, 4-5, 18-19
  1 Peter 2:4-9
  John 14:1-12
[59] Homily given on 29 May 2011

Sixth Sunday of Easter⁶⁰⁶¹
Relationship with God

Relationships are tricky. It's not just that the interaction between people can be complex at times, it's also about understanding the nature of the relationship itself. How do you explain the union of a married couple who have shared a lifetime together? How do you describe the bond of parent and child? What is love? It's complicated, and yet incredibly simple. It involves feelings and emotions, connections and things held in common, values and ideas, time, thoughts and togetherness - a mixture that is difficult to define. Sometimes we find it hard to put our feelings into words, to let others know how important they are to us. Sometimes we don't even know ourselves. How many people are surprised by the depths of their own feeling when they lose someone close to them - through a breakup or a bereavement? You discover that the other person holds a part of you; you might have known it before, but it really comes home to you when it comes to letting go. A part of yourself is wrenched asunder, and we are diminished. Sometimes, when a relative has died, we might have a sense of them being still close to us, still with us, and we might not be sure what that's about.

Today in the gospel Jesus is trying to prepare his disciples for his death, and what would follow it - how he would rise, and then return to the Father. They weren't particularly open to the whole idea, and struggled with it, often rejecting any suggestion that he might die or leave them. Today we see him trying to put words on the relationship that he has with the Father and which we are called to share with them. The Holy Spirit is to be sent, so that in him and through him, we may be enfolded in the life of God. Love is at the heart of it; love is where all of this happens. Jesus tells his

The world cannot accept him, because it neither sees him nor knows him. But you know him, for he lives with you and will be in you. I will not leave you as orphans; I will come to you. Before long, the world will not see me anymore, but you will see me. Because I live, you also will live. On that day you will realize that I am in my Father, and you are in me, and I am in you.

Jn 14:17-20

For personal reflection

God works in you!

followers that in a short while the world will not see him, but they will; then they will understand that he is in the Father, the Father is in him, and he in them and they in him. Here Jesus is putting words on the intimate union with God which we are called to and created for, and struggle to understand. The only behaviour is described as keeping the commandments of Jesus - this is a sign of our love, and a guarantee that we are loved by God.

No less than our human relationships, it's difficult to find words to describe our relationship with God. But it is certainly a level of intimacy that we can hardly dare to imagine. St. Teresa of Avila describes the soul as an interior castle, with one room leading into another, and the presence of God in the innermost room. God dwells within us; we are tabernacles of the Most High, places where God dwells. And yet, we might not be even aware of it, not aware of his presence within us and among us. That presence in each one of us, unites us with one another, bringing about communion among the followers of Christ. Intimacy and intimate relationships are all about degrees of closeness and unity; oftentimes we lack the words to express them. But this should not lead us to lose faith in them or dismiss it all as a strange idea or religious gobbledegook. It's part of our faith, and as we grow in faith and in the presence of the Spirit, hopefully we begin to understand it and experience it more richly.

If we find it hard to put words on what's going on in our human relationships, how much more difficult it is to put words on the inner workings of our relationship with God; but all of these relationships are real. The words of Jesus in the gospel today offer a kind of signpost for us, to help us discover and understand how and where God works within us. As we approach Pentecost, we pray that the Spirit of God may enlighten us and lead us more fully into this life that has been given to us.

---

[60] Acts 8:5-8, 14-17
  Psalm 65:1-7, 16, 20
  I Peter 3:15-18
  John 14:15-21
[61] Homily given on 25 May 2014

Ascension Day
Christ leads humanity into the presence of the Father

One of the things people sometimes ask is why doesn't Christ appear among us now? Why did he leave his disciples after the resurrection and return to the Father? He wasn't bound by space or the limits that are part of our life, why then did he not stay and complete his work here?

Part of the answer to that is that his work was done.

The Ascension marks the completion of the earthly ministry of Christ. This phase of God's mission is ended, and a new one, the next stage, is about to begin with the sending of the Holy Spirit at Pentecost. The Ascension marks the return of the Son to the Father, going back where he started, and with it something else is manifested, another new thing. For the Son of God who came down from heaven, took flesh on earth in the womb of Mary; that human flesh of the Christ didn't come directly from God; it came from Mary. But it is in his human body, risen from the dead, that he returns. This is an extraordinary way to complete the work and mission of God. In returning to the Father in his human form, Christ leads humanity into the presence of the Father. Human flesh enters heaven, and the way is opened for all humanity to follow. Thus, Christ finishes his mission by opening up our destiny to us, revealing to us what lies ahead and where we are to follow, and so his mission here on earth is fulfilled.

There's always a great sense of fulfilment when you finally get a job finished, or even

Go, make disciples of all the nations.

I am with you always; yes, to the end of time.

Mt 28:19,20

FOR PERSONAL REFLECTION

Filled with hope, reflect on how you help make disciples.

complete a certain stage of a project. There's satisfaction at seeing it through, and the even greater satisfaction of having the benefit of the work done. It's always good to finish what we've started.

But there's also a sense in which the work of Christ isn't finished, and I'm sure that the disciples and those who knew him were very confused and maybe even felt abandoned when Jesus ascended into heaven. They had followed him in his days in Galilee and Judaea, leaving their families and work; they had heard him preach about the kingdom of God and saw the signs he worked; they had been with him in Jerusalem in the last days, scattering at his death, but coming together once more when he rose. They had been filled with hope, and had seen all of that hope shattered, and then restored to something new, something beyond their imagination, in their experience of the resurrection. And now Jesus leaves them again. And where was the kingdom of God?

But this time Jesus promised to send the Holy Spirit among them to continue his work and mission, bringing life and hope, and light and joy to all people, the Good News of God's love. We are not abandoned; through the Spirit, God is with us; God is working in us. Christ does not leave us orphans but continues his work in the world through his body, the Church, his people in whom he is present through the Holy Spirit. And we have been sent out by him to bring that Good News to all people.

Today he sends us forth to baptise all peoples in the name of the Father, the Son and the Spirit, just as we're sent out at the end of Mass to witness to Christ and preach. In the power of the Spirit, we go; in the power of the Spirit we carry out the mission entrusted to us. And so in these days before Pentecost, let us ask the Spirit to come upon us once more, to renew us, to renew our parish community, to renew the whole Church, so that the work of Christ may be continued through us in the presence and the power of his Holy Spirit.

Why do Christians baptise people? Why do we witness to our beliefs? Why do we hand on our faith to our children and young people? Why do we send out missionaries to those who do not know Christ? Because Jesus asked us to: "Go, therefore, make disciples of all the nations; baptise them in the name of the Father and of the Son and of the Holy Spirit, and teach them to observe all the commands I gave you." That is why Christians -all Christians, all of us - are called to be missionary. That is why we are told at Mass to go out and proclaim the gospel of the Lord. The words are so familiar, that we might not realise their power or the urgency with which this task is given to us. Having been nourished by the Word of God and celebrated the living Jesus recalling his life, death and resurrection in the Eucharistic memorial, we are sent out to share with others what we have received, just as the first disciples, having been nourished by his word, and having witnessed his life, death and resurrection, were also sent out by him.

Next time you hear those words, let us listen to what we're being asked and let us ask the Spirit of God to fill us, so that next time we gather, we may say "yes, I have witnessed to him; I have preached his word, witnessed to his Good News, and to his presence among us."

In becoming human, God's Son took on an identity with all of humanity, so that in the very definition of what it is to be human, this association with God is key... where Christ leads, we follow.

---

[122] Acts 1:1-11
  Psalm 46(47):2-3,6-9
  Ephesians 1:17-23
  Matthew 28:16-20
[123] Homily given on 1 June 2014

FEAST OF PENTECOST

IN THE SPIRIT OF ST. WILLIBRORD

I'm going to Luxembourg tomorrow to take part in the Dancing Procession or Hopping Procession of St. Willibrord. At this stage, you're probably aware that St Willibrord came from Yorkshire, and when he was 18 or 20, came to Carlow, where he studied at an Anglo-Saxon house in Clonmelsh, probably attached to the monastery at Old Leighlin. He was imbued in the Irish Celtic tradition of spirituality, culture and scholarship, and he was ordained a priest here. After 12 years in Ireland, he led a mission to the Low Countries. The monastic house where he lived in Clonmelsh or Rath Melsigi, as it was known then, had already sent a mission to the Low Countries, but it had returned without success. Willibrord went with 11 others, Irish and Anglo-Saxons, and eventually became the bishop of Utrecht in Holland. He went twice to Rome, once to receive his mandate to preach in those lands, once to be made bishop. He founded a monastery at Echternach, in modern day Luxembourg, and it became very famous for its manuscripts, its school and its life of monastic prayer, until it was closed during the French Revolution. Willibrord travelled quite a bit preaching the gospel in Belgium, Holland, the Frisian islands, Germany, even reaching Denmark. The people of Echternach, where he died, are presenting us with a relic of the saint, which will be contained in a statue, which we'll house over here. Hopefully, the area will be prepared for the shrine next week.

I mention Willibrord not just because 59 of us are going to Luxembourg tomorrow morning, but because of his link with Pentecost. This

"Peace be with you! As the Father has sent me, I am sending you." And with that he breathed on them and said, "Receive the Holy Spirit."

Jn 20:21-22

FOR PERSONAL REFLECTION

Send forth your Spirit, O Lord, and renew the face of the earth.

procession takes place each year on the Tuesday after Pentecost, whenever that occurs. In his life, Willibrord illustrated clearly what the message of Pentecost was about, people of all tongues speaking the word of God, going out to all nations in the energy of the Holy Spirit, to bring the Good News of God's love and forgiveness to the world. There's quite a lot known about St. Willibrord; we know that he healed people, that he forgave them, that he taught them, that he combatted evil and wrongdoing. He lit the flame of faith in their hearts and led them to Christ.

Willibrord is coming back to Carlow in the gift of this relic, and I wonder if this is the influence of the Holy Spirit, sending St. Willibrord on mission once more, back to the land where he was nurtured as a young man? Ireland has become a very secular country very rapidly, and in rejecting the wrongdoing of many churchmen and women, a lot of Irish Catholics have stepped back from the Church entirely and even from God. We have been brainwashed by a culture which presumes that the Church is wrong, no matter what it says. And no one is saying 'stop.'

The Mass doesn't depend on the priest who presides - it is the same sacrifice of Christ offered once for all on Calvary in which we participate at Mass; no matter who the priest is, the Eucharist is the same and our Communion with Christ is the same, yet fewer come. The Holy Spirit is still calling on men and women to witness to the Good News of the Gospel in Ireland, to stand for God. The Church - priests, religious, lay people, men, women, children, all of us as Church - is tasked with the transformation of society and the proclamation of God to all people, each of us in our legitimate sphere, our places of work or education, places of leisure, in the media, in the marketplace, in politics, everywhere. We're not asked to force our beliefs on anyone, but we are called to know what Christ teaches, to witness to that teaching, to live by those beliefs and to challenge others when necessary, and above all to witness to the loving kindness and forgiveness of our God.

The Irish Catholic laity has been described as a sleeping giant: - a large number of people, whose voice is not being heard in Ireland today, maybe because they don't know what to say, maybe because of the wrongs of the past, maybe because they've been hurt and are still bruised, maybe because they see it as the role of the bishops and clergy to speak, maybe because they've lost faith, maybe because they're nervous or afraid, maybe because they're simply not used to us and don't know what to say or do. Faith in this country is in crisis, not just the crisis of vocations, but the crisis that is represented by the large numbers who come for sacraments and never come again, the people who are not at home here, who don't know how to behave or what to do when they arrive for weddings, funerals or different occasions. How is it that young people reared in Catholic homes don't know their prayers?

St. Willibrord comes back to Carlow and to Ireland in the wake of this Pentecost pilgrimage - I think it's a missionary journey, and I pray that his mission among us may help awaken the sleeping giant and rekindle the fire of the Holy Spirit in the hearts of Irish men and women.

---

[62] Acts 2:1-11
  Psalm 103:1, 24, 29-31
  1 Corinthians 12:3-7, 12-13
  John 20:19-23
[63] Homily given on 3 June 2017

Feast of the Most Holy Trinity[6465]
Have life

There's a story told about how St. Augustine was struggling to understand the mystery of the Trinity; he was walking on a beach and he saw a boy in front of him who had dug a hole in the sand and was going out to the sea again and again and bringing some water to pour into the hole. St. Augustine asked him, "What are you doing?" "I'm going to pour the entire ocean into this hole," said the boy. "That is impossible, the whole ocean will not fit in the hole you have made", said St. Augustine. The boy replied, "And you cannot fit the Trinity in your tiny little brain." The story concludes by saying that the boy vanished because St. Augustine had been talking to an angel. Mind you it didn't stop Augustine from his reflection; his work on the Trinity took up no less than 15 books.

But the story pretty much dismisses any attempt we might make to understand the mystery of the Trinity, and instead it points to what is more important - that the Trinity is a mystery that is lived and experienced. The Trinity is about love, the unity that is love and the community that is united in love. We believe that we humans are created in the image and likeness of God; so we are told in the Book of Genesis, and God is one, but yet three persons, and God is love. The fundamental nature of humanity is to be many persons, each one unique and special and different, but all united in love, united in community.

And so our readings today reflect the love of our God, and the ways in which we are called to experience that love and to respond to it. Moses describes God as a God of tenderness and compassion, slow to anger, rich in kindness and faithfulness. This comes from the Book of Exodus in the Old Testament,

For God so loved the world that he gave his one and only Son, that whoever believes in him shall not perish but have eternal life.

Jn 3:16

FOR PERSONAL REFLECTION

Live in God and truly live!

the section of the bible we more often associate with very different images of God. St Paul in the second reading speaks of the God of love and peace, and prays twice that God will be with us. He says: "The God of love and peace will be with you" and "The grace of the Lord Jesus Christ, the love of God and the fellowship of the Holy Spirit be with you all." We still use that greeting at the start of the Mass.

"The Lord be with you." God-with-us, - Emmanuel - Being with God is at the heart of Christian life; we are not called simply to believe in the mystery of the Trinity as something difficult to understand but not having any impact on our lives - no, we're called to live with the Trinity, to live in the Trinity, as members of the Body of Christ, who is one of the persons of the Trinity. Our destiny is to be united with God, and we are called to share the life of God even now. God is with us at every moment of our day. All our prayer is made in his name, - in the name of the Father, Son and Holy Spirit. Our God is not a lonely, distant God far away, and we are never alone, abandoned or deserted - our God is with us, calling us into his life, inviting us as members of the Body of Christ, to live with him and in him.

To live in God is truly to live, - because God is the source of all life; to live in God is truly to love, because God is love and constantly enriches and nurtures our love. The words in the gospel about condemnation are not about condemnation in a judgmental sense, but rather they describe what it is to live without love, to exist in that half-life which is no life, to live without God, the source of life and love. There are many who seek God, but do not know that it is God whom they seek. They will find him, if they look for love and truth and goodness and right. But no more than St. Augustine, none of us will be able to fit the Trinity in our little brains.

---

[64] Exodus 34:4-6, 8-9
   Daniel 3:52-56
   1 Corinthians 13:11-13
   John 3:16-18
[65] Homily given on 15 June 2014

FEAST OF CORPUS CHRISTI
THE BODY AND BLOOD OF CHRIST[6667]
BREAD FROM HEAVEN

There's a beautiful stained-glass window over there (Carlow Cathedral) that depicts the Last Supper. This is one of those occasions where Jesus fed his followers. It wasn't the first time he had done so, but this was special. In fact, Jesus had taken bread on several occasions and fed the crowds, and on two occasions fed them also with fish. Throughout the Old Testament, there are stories of God feeding his people, the most extraordinary being the miracle of the manna in the desert during that time when Moses was leading the people out of slavery in Egypt. "Bread from heaven," the people called it. It's one of the signs of the divine presence - the Lord feeds his people.

But this feeding at the Last Supper was different, because Jesus took the bread, broke it and as he gave it to his disciples he told them that it was his body which would be given for them, and the same with the cup, the wine which he now called the blood of the new covenant, poured out for the forgiveness of sins. And then the command to do this in his memory.

In our gospel today, we see Jesus preparing his followers for this sacred meal, preparing them to receive this new bread which was no ordinary bread, but his flesh. The language he used was very physical - it's almost as if he's deliberately steering away from any tendency to play down the meaning of what he's doing. His flesh is real food; his blood is real drink. The bread he will give is his flesh. For the Jews, flesh was not quite the same as it is for us - it's not just about meat, but it's the life of the person. So the flesh we receive is the life of Christ, physically

"I am the living bread which has come down from heaven. Anyone who eats this bread will live for ever; and the bread that I shall give is my flesh, for the life of the world.
Jn 6:51

FOR PERSONAL REFLECTION

Receive the Body and Blood of Christ.

and spiritually present in us. The people who heard Jesus at that time had great difficulty with this teaching, and many of them left him; some felt that the physicality of his language was tantamount to promoting cannibalism. But that wasn't what he meant. To others, that Christ could be identified with a piece of bread and a cup of wine might seem quite ridiculous; after all they don't change in their appearance or in their taste, but the underlying reality of what they are has changed. Their substance has changed; we call it transubstantiation. Over the centuries people have struggled with this, and many have parted company with the Catholic Church, some even with Christianity, because of it.

There are three things which come to mind when we reflect on the Eucharist, the Bread of Life.

Firstly, when we receive Holy Communion, Christ lives in us; we receive the person of Christ. We might not see him, or feel him or be aware of him, but he is closer to us than we can ever imagine. We are truly privileged to receive Christ into our own bodies, uniting our lives with his in a manner that is both physical and spiritual, and so that time of receiving Communion and afterwards is sacred, truly holy and special.

Secondly, the food that we receive is a communion, not simply with the person of Christ and his life, but also with the offering of himself on the cross and in the resurrection - it is his body and blood that are given up for us, poured out for us, the sacrifice of the new covenant. We share communion with his life, death and resurrection, and through receiving him in the Eucharist, we are caught up in the story of his sacrifice and of his new life: it is present in us. And so we come to share in the fruits of Christ's sacrifice, the forgiveness of sin and the new life of the resurrection.

Thirdly, the food that we receive is the food of heaven. Being united with Christ means that his life, his eternal life is us. We are so closely united with him that we become part of his body and share in his eternal life.

And so, the Communion we receive is not something we take lightly. At one time, reverence and respect for the Eucharist had grown to such an extent that people no longer felt worthy to receive the Body of Christ, and the Church had to insist that Christians receive Communion at least once a year - the Easter Duty. Nor could anyone but the priest touch the host. Since Pius X, that has changed and people are encouraged to receive more frequently, but with familiarity comes greater informality, and oftentimes a lessening of respect and reverence. Our challenge today is to grow not just in our reverence, but in our awareness and appreciation of the God who has sent his Son among us, and who gives himself to us, in all vulnerability in the Communion that we share.

---

[66] Deuteronomy 8:2-3, 14-16
   Psalm 147:12-15, 19-20
   Corinthians 10:16-17
   John 6:51-58
[67] Homily given on 22 June 2014

YEAR A

SUNDAYS IN ORDINARY TIME CONTINUED

Tenth Sunday in Ordinary Time[6869]
Every vocation is a vocation to love

In this year of vocation, we focus on the vocation of marriage during this month of June, praying particularly for those who are called to this vocation – the vast majority of Christian women and men. And we sometimes forget that marriage is a call – it is a call given by the God of Love, experienced in the love one feels for his or her spouse. It is a call to which a person is called to respond with generosity and love. Every vocation is a vocation to love and to service and to witness. These three themes are mentioned on the logo for the year of vocations. In marriage, the witness is to the love of God, to faithfulness, to the presence of God who is love in the lives of men and women. It is a witness to unity, two becoming one in God's love. It is a call to witness to the love of Jesus Christ, who gave his life for all of us out of love. We look to married people to see witnesses to that same life-giving love lived out in society. The call to service is about serving one another, but also about the service of children and family and the wider community. Above all the call to love is predominant. God is love, and there's something extraordinarily beautiful about the love of God made real and concrete, made flesh in the lives of men and women joined in marriage. We learn how to love from our parents. Parents, who are fragile, vulnerable and weak, are called to be the primary vessel of God's love in the lives of their children.

The gospel today tells of the call of Matthew, the tax-collector. Here was a man who had given his life to the service of the state. In doing so, he was despised by his fellow citizens. Tax-collectors were regarded as collaborators with the Romans, but also, because they could keep a percentage of the tax they collected, they were widely regarded as being greedy

As Jesus was walking on, he saw a man named Matthew sitting by the customs house, and he said to him, 'Follow me.' And he got up and followed him.

While he was at dinner in the house it happened that a number of tax collectors and sinners came to sit at the table with Jesus and his disciples. When the Pharisees saw this, they said to his disciples, 'Why does your master eat with tax collectors and sinners?' When he heard this he replied, 'It is not the healthy who need the doctor, but the sick. Go and learn the meaning of the words: What I want is mercy, not sacrifice. And indeed I did not come to call the virtuous, but sinners.'

Mt 9:9-13

FOR PERSONAL REFLECTION

Each vocation involves the struggle to be faithful with the deeper fidelity of love – the fidelity of living each day in love, of choosing to be where you're called to be rather than somewhere else.

Reflecting on these words from the homily, how do they resonate with how you live your call?

and dishonest. Jesus called Matthew at his workplace, in the customs house. He called where he happened to find him. Matthew wasn't at one of his talks; he wasn't at prayer in the synagogue; he was simply at his work when he heard Jesus calling him. And the call was to leave his work, his life, and to follow Jesus. Call always involves leaving something. Those of you who are married know that in committing to that way of life, you had to leave another behind you. Those who have seen their sons and daughters marry know the pain amid the joy, the loss that is involved in seeing them go and make this new life for themselves. It can't have been easy for Matthew to leave his life and to journey into the unknown with this itinerant preacher. He would have been well-off, secure and we know how difficult it can be to leave behind security, the hold that possessions, house, wealth can have. But Matthew leaves it behind to follow Jesus.

Each of us is called to follow Christ. Each vocation – married life, priesthood, single life, religious life, is a call to follow Christ. Each vocation involves the struggle to be faithful with the deeper fidelity of love – the fidelity of living each day in love, of choosing to be where you're called to be rather than somewhere else. We tend to use the language of infidelity in relation to marriage, but it applies to all vocations. Infidelity – lack of faithfulness – is the betrayal involved in choosing self over love, in self-service rather than serving the other. The call to faithfulness is the call to follow Christ as the way and the truth and the life of the love to which we have been asked to give our lives. Pope John Paul spoke of a civilisation of love – this new civilisation is the Christian vision for the world and society in which we live. It is to come into existence in every home, in every community, in every office, in every factory, in each place of work or leisure, every place where people gather. The challenge of building this civilisation of love is ours.

Christ is the source of every vocation – he issues the call in love; he plants the love within us and gives the generosity and the courage to respond. For all who wonder which way in life to choose, why not turn to Christ and ask him – what does he call you to? What gift is he giving you? How is he calling you to love?

---

[68] Hosea 6:3-6
   Psalm 49(50):1,8,12-15
   Romans 4:18-25
   Matthew 9:9-13
[69] Homily given on 1 June 2008

94

ELEVENTH SUNDAY IN ORDINARY TIME⁷⁰⁷¹
HOLDING OUR OPPOSITES TOGETHER

You often find different tensions in religious belief, things that seem to be opposite are held to be true. Perhaps it's just a human characteristic, that we ourselves, our culture, our society, can hold opposites together – that sometimes we're one thing, other times the complete opposite – sometimes outgoing, other times shy or reflective; sometimes honest and upright, other times less than honest; sometimes happy, other times sad. And we hold these tensions within us; both of them may be true, but neither tells the whole story. And we see something of that in the picture that our readings paint for us today. The first reading shows how God called the people of Israel to be his own people. He set them apart from other peoples. "You of all the nations shall be my very own... I will count you a kingdom of priests, a consecrated nation." The people were to be holy, dedicated to God – a priestly people, meaning by that that they would be a people who would represent all others before God and represent God's presence before the rest of the world. The gospel however shows us that this priestly people is not set apart forever; instead we see the disciples of Christ sent out to be his witnesses and to proclaim his coming, sent out initially to the people of Israel and later sent out to the whole world. That tension is one which has been part of the Church since the beginning. Our Church emerged from the people of Israel, who had a very strong sense of being separate from other peoples, the chosen people which belonged only to the Lord; but we also had this strong mandate, a commandment to go out to all the world and to proclaim his message.

A lot of issues are raised here in these readings; they have many implications for us, for our faith and for our Church. Firstly, we are called

When Jesus saw the crowds, he felt sorry for them because they were harassed and dejected, like sheep without a shepherd. Then he said to his disciples, 'The harvest is rich, but the labourers are few, so ask the Lord of the harvest to send labourers to his harvest.'

Mt 9:36-38

FOR PERSONAL REFLECTION

How have you shared your faith this week?
Reflect on the ways you have witnessed to your faith.

to be the Lord's own people; we are a priestly people. The Lord our God is the source of our life, the source of our hope and our love. Without him, we are nothing and our faith and our witness are empty and ring hollow. And so there is an urgency about being with the Lord, learning to know him better, spending time in prayer and reflection and spiritual reading.

Secondly, our faith is not just for us; we are called to share it, to witness to it. It's not something personal or private – it's to be shared. That's quite a difficult thing for many in our society today. We see religion being consigned to the realm of the personal and the private. You can believe what you like, as long as it doesn't interfere in the workings of society or impinge in any way on others. That's not what Christ called us to do. We are witnesses in the world; we are his presence to the world – the body of Christ, sent to bring the good news to all, to bring healing and hope to a broken world. We cannot hide our light under a bushel.

Furthermore, we are called by name. We see how the apostles were called by name and sent to the people of Israel. The word apostle means "sent" – they are the ones sent out – missionaries – just as we are sent out at the end of every Mass to bear witness to what we have experienced – "Go in peace to love and serve the Lord." To be a disciple is to be a follower of Jesus; to be an apostle is to be sent. We are called to be something of both. And we too are called by name; you notice at baptism and again at Confirmation, the candidates are named, called by name, known to God, special to him, each one with a particular calling and mission in life. We are his, sent out to a world that does not know him and which refuses to acknowledge him.

"The harvest is rich, but the labourers are few, so ask the Lord of the harvest to send labourers to his harvest." In this year of vocation, we ask that each one of us grow in awareness of the calling that God is giving to us; we ask him to send labourers into the harvest, men and women, lay, religious and priests – to witness to his love and to proclaim his presence in the world of today.

---

[70] Exodus 19:2-6
  Psalm 99(100):2-3,5
  Romans 5:6-11
  Matthew 9:36-10:8
[71] Homily given on 15 June 2008

TWELFTH SUNDAY IN ORDINARY TIME⁷²⁷³
TIMES OF FEAR

In the gospel today, Jesus reassures the disciples at a time when they are hesitant and afraid. They are aware that the future will not be easy for them, perhaps Jesus has been speaking to them about his forthcoming suffering and death; many times, he warned his disciples that following him would bring them suffering and pain. He appears to be teaching them in secret "what I say to you in the dark, tell in the daylight." This is a time of fear for them, a time of loneliness, a time when the disciples found it difficult to understand God's love, and how God could be with them when to all intents and purposes, he seemed to have deserted them.

Jesus assures us that we are loved by God and we are precious to him. He knows us intimately, better than we imagine, better we know ourselves. "Every hair on you head has been counted. So, there is no need to be afraid; you are worth more than hundreds of sparrows." So, in our times of fear and loneliness, the times of terror that the first reading speaks of, we have the confidence that God is with us, that he knows us and that he loves us. We take this granted to such an extent that frequently it doesn't make any impact on us at all. And yet there are strong symbols of this abiding presence in our faith, strong signs that God is faithful and that his love for us endures. One of those signs is the sacrament of marriage. You remember the story of the wedding feast of Cana, how Jesus turned the water into wine – wine is a sign of the kingdom; Jesus is saying to us that marriage is no longer something earthly, something of water; it is a sign of the presence of the kingdom – a sign that God

Jesus instructed the Twelve as follows: 'Do not be afraid,'

Mt 10:26

FOR PERSONAL REFLECTION

Reflect on a time when fear and hesitancy drove you towards God and give thanks for the support you received.

97

is with us. In the love of husband and wife, God is present. God is love; whoever lives in love live in God. Those who have made the commitment of their lives to one another in love are bound as one in the unity of God's love – they are wrapped in God's love. At the wedding ceremony, the priest asks that the Lord may seal the love of the husband and wife. So, the marriage of a woman and a man is a sign of God's love; in and through Christian marriage, God's love becomes present to the world; God becomes present to the world through them. God gives the gift of his love to the husband through his wife, and to the wife through her husband.

God is the giver of life, and his love is life-giving, and so the love of husband and wife in Christian marriage cooperates with God's life-giving love in so far as the man and wife are naturally fertile, as their love gives life to their children.

There are very different understandings of marriage in society today – the legal contract that exists between married people, the marriage customs of different religions that are now more common, cultural differences. In the midst of this changing reality, the specifically Christian dimension to Christian marriage needs to be recognised and nurtured; Christian marriage is not the same as other forms of marriage. It is a relationship of two people sealed by God, who gives his life to them, and is faithful to them throughout their lives. They are called to witness to this abiding love; they are called to be a sign of Christ's love. We remember that Christ loved us so much that he gave his life for us; the vocation of marriage is a call to witness to this love as husband and wife give their live to one another; it is a call to mutual service and self-giving.

The other great sacrament of God's loving presence among us is the Eucharist – and it's so similar to marriage. This is the ritual that Jesus gave us so that we could continue to share in his gift of his life for us. As he gives us the bread of life, he says "this is my body, given up for you." This is the gift of his life, of his body for us. These words have a special meaning for married couples, for they too give the gift of their lives to one another, symbolised and celebrated in the giving of their bodies.

The Christian understanding of marriage often seems far removed from the day-to-day reality of people's lives. But it shouldn't be removed from it; rather, it should be a source of nourishment and inspiration. After all, at the heart of our faith is our belief in the Word made flesh, our belief that God can be present in the ordinary human experiences and realities. The vocation of marriage is to discover that divine presence and to witness to it in Christian marriage. In this month of June, the Year of Vocation calls us to focus on Christian marriage. We give thanks to God for the married couples who teach us how to love, who witness to divine love and strive to make it present in the experiences of every day.

---

[72] Jeremiah 20:10-13
   Psalm 68(69):8-10,14,17,33-35
   Romans 5:12-15
   Matthew 10:26-33
[73] Homily given on 22 June 2008

Thirteenth Sunday in Ordinary Time[7475]
World Meeting of Families

Next year we welcome the World Meeting of Families to Dublin, and with it a probable visit to Ireland by Pope Francis. Families from all over the world are invited to take part, to be part of a week-long experience. It's an opportunity to meet families from different parts of the world, a chance to explore and share and learn, but above all, to celebrate family life in all its various forms and shapes. Family is hard to define, but as Archbishop Diarmuid Martin put it, we mightn't be able to define a family, but we all know one when we see one. It's not just about the conventional father, mother, children model - there are and always have been families with different shapes. In preparation for the World Meeting of Families, the icon of the Holy Family sits here, calling us to come to the home of Nazareth and to learn from it, to recognise how this family embraced the presence of God into the heart of its family life, how it was shaped by the presence of God's love, and how it grew to accept mission, suffering, death. A special icon for the World Meeting of Families will visit Carlow next year.

Our diocese is holding a diocesan picnic to mark the beginning of preparations for the World Meeting of Families, to be held exactly a year ahead on August 27 this year at Punchestown Racecourse. It's hoped that families from all over the diocese will come together, extended families, young families, older families, single people, all of us are part of a family. You might have seen the posters around.

It's interesting how we talk about God in terms that refer to family relationships, Father and the Son. We call Mary the Mother of God. Because

'Anyone who prefers father or mother to me is not worthy of me. Anyone who prefers son or daughter to me is not worthy of me. Anyone who does not take his cross and follow in my footsteps is not worthy of me. Anyone who finds his life will lose it; anyone who loses his life for my sake will find it.

'Anyone who welcomes you welcomes me; and those who welcome me welcome the one who sent me.

'Anyone who welcomes a prophet will have a prophet's reward; and anyone who welcomes a holy man will have a holy man's reward.

'If anyone gives so much as a cup of cold water to one of these little ones because he is a disciple, then I tell you solemnly, he will most certainly not lose his reward.'

Mt 10:37-42

For personal reflection

Do something special for and with your family this week.

we're created in God's image and likeness, family exists - that's how God is, God's very nature - sharing things in common, bound by a spirit of love, united to one another by something deep within. We sometimes refer to Church as the family of God. God is our Father and we are his children, for in baptism we are grafted into Christ and become sons and daughters, in and through the One who is the Father's only begotten Son. And so, as St. Paul reminds us, we too are called to live a new life, to rise from death to take our place with our Father.

Strange then, that the gospel begins with such a stern warning "Anyone who prefers father or mother to me is not worthy of me. Anyone who prefers son or daughter to me is not worthy of me," and these words come from Christ, whom we like to associate with the most gentle, loving and caring attitudes. This jars a bit perhaps. What we have here is typical of the exaggeration which was common in Jewish culture and which we're given to a bit ourselves. How big was the fish you caught? It was this big. How much should you love God; you should love him this much, more than even your own family and your own self. It's not about making choices, it's about remembering and learning just how important God is to us, just how significant it is for us to follow Christ - it's as important as family, and Christ is family, closer to us than even our mothers or our spouses, our children, our fathers, or siblings.

It's not an either/or choice between family and God, either family or God. It's about recognising the presence of God in our families, in those closest to us. It's about the fundamental belief that God is love, present in all human love, the source of all human love, holding all human love and all human beings in the palm of his hand.

And sometimes Christ makes demands on us that call on us to choose him first. It might involve a moral choice, a question of right and wrong; it might be something else. Last Sunday I was at the ordination of Fr David Vard in Newbridge, a young man who after a long period of discernment and preparation, has chosen to give his life to God and to the service of people, putting the family of God before his own family. That might seem a strange choice for a young man to make, but when Christ calls and you recognise the truth of his call, it is the right response. The discipline involved in being a disciple is not always an easy one.

The gospel today is about recognising that God is fundamental to everything else, the foundation of all other loves, and so God is first, as his presence underlies even our own existence. We are built on God's love; we grow in God's love. We, together with our families, live and move and have our being in and through God's loving presence, and in loving others, in welcoming others, we love and welcome God.

[74] 2 Kings 4:8-11,13-16
   Psalm 88(89):2-3,16-19
   Romans 6:3-4,8-11
   Matthew 10:37-42
[75] Homily given on 22 June 2008

What does your heart most truly desire? What is your deepest longing? What yearning makes your heart sing when it finds something that approaches fulfilment? What is it that makes you realise that your heart is more than a piece of flesh beating inside you, but something that truly lives, a spiritual presence in the depths of your being? Often, it is in the hungers of the body that this longing is most urgently expressed - we feel it in a piece of music that truly touches us and moves us, at a profound level, be it the poetry of a Bob Dylan, a Bruce Springsteen, Coldplay or the soaring heights of opera and the classics. We know it in nature or in things of beauty, in the mountains, lakes and valleys, the seas and skies, in sculpture, painting, whenever we have to pause and wonder. It expresses itself in our cravings for food, for drink, in our sexual desires, in our need to be with others. It is a desire that encompasses all our desires but which they can only partly fulfil, for as St. Augustine famously said, "our hearts are restless until they rest in God." All these human longings are but facets of that innate, instinctive longing for the One who created us. All our hunger for love, for fulfilment, for union with others, expresses our deepest hunger for the love of God and union with him. The first part of that quote from Augustine "you have made us for yourself O Lord, and our hearts are restless until they rest in you."

Faith comes easy to little ones; they know that they are loved by God and they trust him implicitly; perhaps because it's not so long since they were just a light in his eyes. As we get older, life gets more complicated and we forgot the simplicity of our childlike faith. A classmate of mine used to remind us that Christ called us to be child-like, not childish - there is a difference. Again and again, Christ places the example of a child before his disciples, and says, "this is how you should be." The canonisation

Jesus exclaimed, 'I bless you, Father, Lord of heaven and of earth, for hiding these things from the learned and the clever and revealing them to mere children. Yes, Father, for that is what it pleased you to do. Everything has been entrusted to me by my Father; and no one knows the Son except the Father, just as no one knows the Father except the Son and those to whom the Son chooses to reveal him.

'Come to me, all you who labour and are overburdened, and I will give you rest. Shoulder my yoke and learn from me, for I am gentle and humble in heart, and you will find rest for your souls. Yes, my yoke is easy and my burden light.'

Mt 11:25-30

For personal reflection

What does your heart most truly desire? What is your deepest longing?

this year of the children of Fatima, Jacinta and Francesco, the apparitions to the young Bernadette in Lourdes, where our diocese will travel next Sunday; - all of these testify to the power of the faith of children. It's something we should not deny to our young people, and many in society would like to deny that faith to them.

Jesus praises his Father for revealing his mysteries to children, when the clever and the learned are blind to them. And then he calls on us all to come to him, to come to his heart, to take refuge and shelter in his heart, for there, we will find rest. We will find rest there and only there, because this is the heart of God. This is the source of love, the Sacred Heart, the living heart of Christ, the heart that was opened for the world on the cross when Jesus gave the gift of his life out of love for us. Cardinal Newman's motto was "cor ad cor loquitur", meaning heart speaks unto heart. It was the theme of Pope Benedict's visit to England in 2010, when he beatified Cardinal Newman. We are called by Christ to discover our hunger for him in the deepest longings of our hearts. We are called by Christ to come to him, to rest in him, to find that those longings and hungers and yearnings are fulfilled and calmed and tamed and directed to their proper purpose when we come to him. We are called to a union of hearts, which is what prayer is really about, as our heart resonates in the heart of Christ, and his heart beats in us.

We use so many words in our prayer; we say prayers. Parrots can say prayers, but to truly pray, we need more than the words. Prayer is an activity of the heart - the words simply lead the way. The deepest prayer is contemplative, and we may reach it only occasionally, as our minds are too busy, too distracted. This is the prayer we make in silence, when we go into the secret chamber of our hearts and sit with God and allow him to fill us. It can come at the end of another type of prayer, perhaps when we pour out our needs, our worries before him, and then stop and listen and simply be. It can come at the end of Mass, as we stop our minds and be silently aware of the presence of Christ living in us, the Eucharist, come to make his home in us. It can come at any time, when we are struck still by something that takes our breathe away - music, nature, people, loves and our heart turns to the One who is the origin of them all. Our God has created us for himself; we are loved; we are wanted; we are beautiful in his eyes, as we are. There is no need to hide before him, no need to be afraid that we are not good enough, no need to run away or to deny anything. Just come before him, and be still and know that there is a place for you in the living heart of God.

---

[76] Zechariah 9:9-10
    Psalm 144(145):1-2,8-11,13b-14
    Romans 8:9,11-13
    Matthew 11:25-30
[77] Homily given on 9 July 2017

As you sow, so shall you reap, goes the old saying, originally from St. Paul's letter to the Galatians. The story in the gospel today expands it a bit, giving us the example of seed that is sown in different places and the results of the harvest. We're probably not surprised to see the seed at the edge of the path falling away; we're well aware that there are people who seem utterly resistant to anything of the Spirit, allergic to faith or religion. We're also familiar with the phenomenon of faith that disappeared with the Celtic Tiger; prosperity and riches choked the life from it. And we also know very well how it can happen that a flourishing faith can die away when certain challenges appear; the scandals in the Church led many to question, not just the Church, but the message that it proclaimed, and they did real damage to people's faith. Today faith is under attack from all sides; in certain circles there's a presumption that you don't go to Mass, don't pray and don't believe, and many people keep the practice of their faith a secret from their work colleagues and even their friends.

Faith needs deep roots to survive; even things like illness, bereavement, relationship issues, financial hardships, can quench faith if its roots are not sufficiently deep. On the other hand, those things can actually strengthen it too, just as pruning is good for the health of plants. It's hard to know how deep our faith actually is; some would say that in Ireland, faith is widespread, but superficial, that we don't have a deep faith. Others would say that its very endurance here is evidence of a deeply held belief. I think myself, that while faith has endured, the challenges that it meets today call for vigilance about faith, attention to

Jesus left the house and sat by the lakeside, but such large crowds gathered round him that he got into a boat and sat there. The people all stood on the beach, and he told them many things in parables.

He said, 'Imagine a sower going out to sow. As he sowed, some seeds fell on the edge of the path, and the birds came and ate them up. Others fell on patches of rock where they found little soil and sprang up straight away, because there was no depth of earth; but as soon as the sun came up they were scorched and, not having any roots, they withered away. Others fell among thorns, and the thorns grew up and choked them. Others fell on rich soil and produced their crop, some a hundredfold, some sixty, some thirty. Listen, anyone who has ears!'

Mt 13:1-9

For personal reflection

Listening to the words of Scripture for this Sunday, reflect on how your faith is thriving.

those things that challenge it, and a deep commitment to nourishing it, strengthening it and helping it to grow.

So how can we do that? The parable speaks of good soil; how can we be that good soil that welcomes the seed of faith and provides a suitable environment for it to flourish? Well, the traditional ways are prayer, fasting and almsgiving.

Prayer is not just about saying prayers; it's about the awareness of God's presence among us; it's about deepening our understanding of our faith through scripture, meditation and spiritual reading. It's about spending time in silence and in quiet before the Blessed Sacrament; it's about pilgrimages and retreats. It's about investing time and energy into our relationship with God.

Fasting is doing without something, depriving our bodies of food or drink. But that's only part of it. It's about leading a healthy lifestyle that is respectful of ourselves and of our environment. Fasting is about curbing our desires - for wealth, for clothes, food, music, television, internet, games, sport. It's about moderation, balance, and at times, doing without some of the things that give us pleasure or amusement so that our character can be deepened and can develop.

Almsgiving is about generosity to those in need, giving what we have to those who have less. But it's also about sharing our time, our energy, our love - engaging with the community in which we live. It's about offering our support and our help to others, giving of ourselves as well as of our possessions.

All of these things help to deepen our character and lead us into a healthier way of living, a way of life where we can welcome God's Word and our faith can deepen and grow. Today is a day to ask ourselves about our own faith. How is it, strong and thriving, or confused, or weak, or just hanging in there? The Word of God can nurture our faith, and our whole lives; it brings a whole new dimension to our life and work. Christ challenges us to receive the Word of God into a soil where it may flourish and thrive. We are the soil; so let us do the spade-work so that God may find a home in us, where faith may grow and deep roots develop.

---

[78] Zechariah 9:9-10
Psalm 64(65):10-14
Romans 8:18-23
Matthew 13:1-23
[79] Homily given on 13 July 2014

Sixteenth Sunday in Ordinary Time[8081]
Life's lessons

One of the lessons we all have to learn in life is about consequences - there are consequences to our actions and our words, which may be good and sometimes aren't. But one way or the other, we have to live with those consequences and respond to whatever they may be. Sometimes we have to live with the consequences of the words or actions of others, they can't be undone either; again, that may be to our benefit, but sometimes they're not, and we can find ourselves feeling angry and hard- done-by, even resentful. There's a bit of a myth that life can be anything that we want it to be, that we can be anything we want to be, but inevitably there are limits to our choices and our abilities, which restrict the possibilities open to us. So, in life we learn to pick ourselves up, and get on with it, to work around the more unfavourable circumstances and consequences and do the best we can.

The parable of the darnel offers a way of looking at the limits and restrictions of life. The weed grows among the good crop, sown by an enemy, and the owner of the field has to put up with them, let them grow, so that the good seed is not lost in trying to undo the consequences of the sowing of the darnel.

In comparing the kingdom of heaven to the field in which the weeds have been sown among the wheat, Jesus invites us to consider how many sad and unfortunate circumstances are part of life, how many sinful actions and consequences are part of our experience. Addictions, bad temper, dishonesty - the personal flaws which cause so much misery not just to those who suffer from them, but also to their families and friends - these are weeds among the good crop of

'The sower of the good seed is the Son of Man. The field is the world; the good seed is the subjects of the kingdom; the darnel, the subjects of the evil one; the enemy who sowed them, the devil; the harvest is the end of the world; the reapers are the angels. Well then, just as the darnel is gathered up and burnt in the fire, so it will be at the end of time. The Son of Man will send his angels and they will gather out of his kingdom all things that provoke offences and all who do evil, and throw them into the blazing furnace, where there will be weeping and grinding of teeth. Then the virtuous will shine like the sun in the kingdom of their Father. Listen, anyone who has ears!'

Mt 13:38-43

For personal reflection

The love of God is more powerful than the greatest evil.

Reflect on the times you have experienced this revelation.

our life. Why can we not escape them? The parable asks us to be patient; indeed the first reading reminds us that our God is greater than anything else, that he cares for everything, that his mercy and judgement are lenient, so we need never fear his justice because it is always accompanied by his mercy and love for sinners. And realistically, that includes all of us, for we all struggle with the consequences of personal failure, sometimes petty, sometimes greater.

The darnel sown among the wheat refers not just to the circumstances of our individual lives, but also to the problems in the wider spheres of society and the world. The conflicts in Palestine, Syria, Iraq, Ukraine and in many African countries remind us that among the many good and beautiful things and places in our world, the weeds of hatred, suspicion, greed, envy among others, poison the lives of people and result in horrendous consequences and loss of life, such as those unfortunate people who died in Ukraine while flying from Amsterdam to Kuala Lumper and the many who have lost their lives in Israel and Gaza. The economic collapse caused by greed had devastating consequences for innocent people. The injustices of society, the illnesses which afflict people, the natural disasters, all of these are weeds among the wheat of our world.

Jesus offers us three parables about the kingdom of God today. The second, the parable of the mustard seed is about small beginnings - it encourages us not to be afraid to make small changes, to do little things which may grow, may have wonderful consequences of their own. Mother Teresa once wrote that God does not want us to do great things, but small things with great love. Another Teresa, St. Therese of Lisieux, wrote about the Little Way of love, in which no action is too small or insignificant to be offered to God as an offering of love. This is the way of the mustard seed.

The third parable, the yeast in flour, describes how the witness of some individuals can transform the environment in which they live. So, take heart; the love of God is more powerful than the greatest evil. We are called to live in that love, to be nourished by it, and animated and motivated by it, to be the witnesses for the kingdom, the presence of God's love in the world today.

---

[80] Wisdom 12:13,16-19
  Psalm 85(86):5-6,9-10,15-16
  Romans 8:26-27
  Matthew 13:1-23
[81] Homily given on 20 July 2014

SEVENTEENTH SUNDAY IN ORDINARY TIME[8283]
WHY DID WE CHOOSE THIS LIFE?

One of the questions people ask the clergy is why we choose the life we do - why priesthood, when there are so many other ways of life to choose, more lucrative, less demanding, a life offering the possibility of marriage and family. There are many reasons why you choose another way. For me, it was as if I discovered that the love of God is something that is immeasurable, immense, beyond all are you can ever imagine or desire. I remember when I was about six, visiting the church at home during exposition of the Blessed Sacrament, and being aware that there was something really significant going on in the depth of the silence - the presence of God was almost palpable. As a youngster looking at what I would do in later life, it seemed that as we come from God at the beginning of our lives and return to God at the end of our lives, so God has to be significant to our existence at every moment in between; there's no time when we're not called to respond to him. Not even for an instant are we outside the reach of his love; there is no time when God is not relevant to us. God's presence, God's love to me as a 17-year-old seemed priceless beyond measure and it still does today. I might not have used the images of the pearl of great price or the treasure in the field, but this evening they seem quite appropriate.

Setting out on the priesthood 26 years ago full of idealism and full of life, giving everything to God, was the most natural and normal thing to do. There could be no other response to his love. It didn't feel as if any great sacrifice had to be made to follow Christ; it was a joy to do so; it was a natural response, the fulfilment of everything that I believed in. As the prophet Nehemiah prayed "May the joy

Jesus said to the crowds, 'The kingdom of heaven is like treasure hidden in a field which someone has found; he hides it again, goes off happy, sells everything he owns and buys the field.

'Again, the kingdom of heaven is like a merchant looking for fine pearls; when he finds one of great value he goes and sells everything he owns and buys it.

'Again, the kingdom of heaven is like a dragnet cast into the sea that brings in a haul of all kinds. When it is full, the fishermen haul it ashore; then, sitting down, they collect the good ones in a basket and throw away those that are no use. This is how it will be at the end of time: the angels will appear and separate the wicked from the just to throw them into the blazing furnace where there will be weeping and grinding of teeth.

Mt 13:44-50

FOR PERSONAL REFLECTION

Reflect on your journey in life – *have you understood?*

of the Lord be our strength." That joy has been part of my life every day, so much of it mediated through the people that I've been privileged to work with and serve. I've found it in abundance here in Carlow, and I'm grateful to God and to all of you for the privilege of spending 17 happy years here in Carlow, firstly as chaplain in IT Carlow from 2000 until 2005, as curate from 2005 to 2006 and then as Administrator from 2006 onwards. And it has indeed been a privilege and an honour to minister at the Cathedral.

In these years, this parish has had its share of ups and downs. We've celebrated weddings, funerals, baptisms, First Communions and Confirmations. We've been through occasions of festivity and of tragedy. We've had ordinations to priesthood, diaconate and the episcopacy. We have marked the coming of two bishops. We celebrated 175 years of Carlow Cathedral. In the first year I came, the relics of St. Therese of Lisieux came to visit Carlow Cathedral; in the year I leave, the relic of St. Willibrord has come to stay. So many events, so much life, too much to mention, so much of it focussed on this building. I've been inspired by the extraordinary faith and commitment of many parishioners, and have learned so much from the many people I've worked with on lots of different committees, as well as the various priests, Parish Staff and CE scheme participants. Thank you.

These years in Carlow have been very special and it has certainly been a privilege to be part of this community. So much so, that I'm far more aware of the cost of discipleship. It's never easy to leave. Following Christ and the path that he chooses involves new beginnings, new adventures certainly, but it also means leaving behind a life, and network of support and friendship, and everything that is familiar. I do so with thanksgiving for having had this precious time. The merchant had to sell everything he had in order to possess the pearl; the one who finds the treasure sells everything to buy the field. As I leave Carlow, I am conscious that I do so with the support, friendship and prayer of this community. This is what Christ calls me to. Spare a thought today for the one who owns the field and does not know that there is a treasure hidden within. Spare a thought for those who have not discovered the joy of Christ's love in their lives. Remember that the mission of Christ belongs to us all. May the joy of the Lord be your strength.

I'm grateful to God and to all of you for making me so welcome in Carlow, over the last 17 years. You have ministered to me far more than I have to you; you have inspired me by your witness, your generosity, courage and dedication.

Four people have worked for the parish for the whole of the 17 years I've been here, our sacristans Billy Lawlor and Michael Townsend, who are incredibly dedicated and generous in their commitment; our housekeeper Bernie Boyd who has minded me and many other clergy, and made our home in the Presbytery a very happy and smooth running establishment and our Parish Sister, Sr. Dolores.

I stand in sheer awe at the dedication of Sr. Dolores, who has been a constant presence in the Cathedral; she is a tremendous support and one of the hardest workers I've ever met.

As administrator here, I've worked with five curates; when I remarked to someone that having had five curates, I might get a reputation, the response came quickly "you have one already." I'd like to wish Fr. Ruairi well in his new position. I know that he has all the gifts and more that he will need here. He has been a great friend and I know that he will be an excellent Administrator here in Carlow.

Abbeyleix will be a big change, but by all accounts, it's a very friendly place. I succeed Fr. Ger Ahern as Parish Priest there; it will be my third time to succeed him.

For what has been THANKS

To what will be YES

---

[82] 1 Kings 3:5,7-12
    Psalm 118(119):57,72,76-77,127-130
    Romans 8:28-30
    Matthew 13:44-52
[83] Homily given on 30 July 2017

Eighteenth Sunday in Ordinary Time⁸⁴⁸⁵

Families suffer

Over the summer, Carlow has seen far more loss of life than any community should have to face. Parents, families and the entire community have been devastated by the loss of young lives. In our country, tragic death has become commonplace, so that people are less shocked by the deaths of young people than we would have been a number of years ago. Many things are blamed - poor mental health, drugs, loneliness, isolation, Facebook, the lack of genuine communication and the inability to talk about our troubles. Who knows? Every story is different, but families suffer.

Today we are reminded of the incredible love that our God has for us. Nothing, we are told, can come between us and the love of Christ - nothing - no trouble, no worry, no persecution (or bullying), no recession, or lack of food or clothing, or even violence - nothing can come between us and Christ's love. Not even death. Christ is the friend who is with us always, whose love for us never changes. Even if we disappoint him or abandon him, his love remains. Today our readings invite us to come to him; come and receive what truly nourishes. The prophet Isaiah says in the first reading "Come to the water all you who are thirsty; though you have no money, come! Buy corn without money and eat, and at no cost, wine and milk." Why then do we waste our lives on worthless things, and then have to suffer the consequences of our experiences, when Christ offers us what is truly life-giving? Isaiah says, "Why spend money on what is not bread, your wages on what fails to satisfy?" Christ is the true bread, the bread of life, the bread that offers the nourishment of a life that knows no end. "Listen and your soul will live," the prophet says.

When evening came, the disciples went to him and said, 'This is a lonely place, and the time has slipped by; so send the people away, and they can go to the villages to buy themselves some food.' Jesus replied, 'There is no need for them to go: give them something to eat yourselves.' But they answered 'All we have with us is five loaves and two fish.' 'Bring them here to me' he said. He gave orders that the people were to sit down on the grass; then he took the five loaves and the two fish, raised his eyes to heaven and said the blessing. And breaking the loaves handed them to his disciples who gave them to the crowds. They all ate as much as they wanted, and they collected the scraps remaining; twelve baskets full. Those who ate numbered about five thousand men, to say nothing of women and children.

Mt 14:15-21

For personal reflection

Sit quietly, *Listen* and feel *your soul live.*

112

We are invited to the table of the Lord, and we come here to eat the bread of life, the Body of Christ. Here Christ offers us his very self, taking the bread, giving thanks for it, breaking it, giving it to the people, just as he did at the Last Supper, just as he did at the lakeshore. The abundance of the feeding in the gospel points to the extraordinary and extravagant love of our God. We are invited, and so are many others who have not responded to this invitation, to come and eat the food that endures, to be part of the communion of Christ's body, united with him and with one another through the one bread, the living presence of Christ, which is shared among us. At the end of our Mass, we are told to go out and to proclaim the gospel of the Lord, or to go in peace, glorifying the Lord in our lives. We need to take that seriously, going out and offering this invitation to others, young people and old people, to come and be nourished, to be fed with food of life at the table of the Lord. We need to take seriously our role as disciples, followers of his, witnesses to his message, a message of life and hope and joy. We need to go out and assure our families, our neighbours, our colleagues of the immense love that our God has for them, the incredible friendship that he offers them, and to invite them to come and be part of it, to be nourished, so that in those days when life is dark and hope seems far away, they will know the truth of today's second reading - that nothing can come between us and the love of God made visible in Jesus Christ.

First reading - the invitation is warm, generous, and heartfelt. It is given freely and it asks for nothing in return. It recognises the poverty of the guest; it opens our eyes to look at how we have squandered our lives. Second reading - reassurance - God's love is greater than anything. Gospel - need to get away, after bereavement - need to pray, to regroup, to be together - time-out. But the need of the crowds is greater. The tender concern of Jesus. Messianic generosity, feeding his people.

In the past weeks we have been horrified by the images of war that have crossed our tv screens, images of injured children, images of families torn apart, houses destroyed, lives shattered. These images have come from Gaza, but not just from Gaza. Some of them are from Africa, from the Ukraine, from so many troubled parts of our world that we can scarcely take it in. As an elderly sister used to say, "you couldn't have grief for it all." Our world still struggles to feed its young, while the problem of overfeeding - obesity - is prevalent too. Famine, disease and unrest - all make for unhappiness, insecurity, injury and death.

And yet today we receive a warm generous invitation to come and be fed, an invitation to come and drink, to come to the Lord and be nourished. The

Gospel fulfils that invitation, as we see Christ feeding the hungry, nourishing those in need of sustenance. And we give thanks for the plenty that we have, yes - even the least well off in a time of recession, - the abundance that we in the developed world have been born into. But what about all the others? What about those who live in lands where water is scarce and the corn does not grow? What about crops destroyed by famine or warfare? Does God not feed them? Does he love them less and us more?

The second reading tells us that nothing can separate us from the love of God. St. Paul lists many things, things that seem insurmountable obstacles to God's love - trouble, worry, persecution, attack, being without food or clothes, not even death can separate us from the love of God. You might wonder why Paul bothers mentioning them, especially the need for food, since God has promised to feed his people.

Then we remember that Jesus said, "I am the bread of life. If anyone eats this bread, he will live forever and the bread that I will give is my flesh which I will give for the life of the world." Of all the different types of hunger, Jesus offers bread to satisfy the deepest hunger of all, and the life that he gives conquers death. "Listen," the prophet says, "and your soul shall live." So the sufferings of the world remain, but they cannot separate us from God's love; St Paul says that they are the trials through which we triumph through the power of the God who loves us.

We often find it hard today to get our heads around the suffering of the innocent, and to understand it when we see the absolute desperation of people - those who suffer from mental illness, those who feel trapped in unhappy and unhealthy relationships, those who live with poverty and financial burdens. It's not as if God is saying "these don't matter." What he's saying is something deeper, that our experience of suffering loses its immense significance in the face of God. Human beings can find the strength to cope with all of these things when they live in the presence and the power of God.

---

[84] Isaiah 55:1-3
Psalm 144(145):8-9,15-18
Romans 8:35,37-39
Matthew 14:13-21
[85] Homily given on 3 August 2014

Nineteenth Sunday in Ordinary Time[8687]

"Lord! Save me!"

The most honest and heartfelt words in scripture must surely be the cry of Peter as he sinks into the cold, wet and stormy waters of Lake Galilee "Lord! Save me!" These words are probably the most profound prayer that humans ever utter, and, let's face it, it's a prayer we all find ourselves making at one time or another – the prayer of desperation, knowing ourselves to be sinking with nothing to cling to, out of our depth, frightened, even terrified. "Lord, save me!" is the prayer we make when we have nowhere else to turn, when only God can retrieve the situation, when we have tried everything else and have come face to face with utter failure. Only he can rescue us or help us cope with it, or give us strength.

And it is Peter who makes that frantic cry in today's gospel. Peter is the disciple that we identify with most of all, perhaps because we know a bit more about him than about the others, or because we identify with his humanity, his impulsiveness, his failure, his eagerness to help, and the speed at which he gets his come-uppance; in one form or another, we've all been there. And yet it is Peter whom Christ chose to be the Rock on which he would build his Church. Peter is the principle of unity, yet he is flawed and sometimes sinful. Above all others, it is the witness of his presence as Christ's apostle that reminds us that God chooses what is weak and sinful and can use it to witness to the power of his transforming love. Those who are weakest know their need of God. It's in our failure, even more than in our successes, that we recognise our dependence on him; and so it is then that we invite him in, allowing his grace to work in us and through us. Those who have it all together have no need of God, for they

In the fourth watch of the night he went towards them, walking on the lake, and when the disciples saw him walking on the lake they were terrified. 'It is a ghost' they said, and cried out in fear. But at once Jesus called out to them, saying, 'Courage! It is I! Do not be afraid.' It was Peter who answered. 'Lord,' he said 'if it is you, tell me to come to you across the water.' 'Come' said Jesus. Then Peter got out of the boat and started walking towards Jesus across the water, but as soon as he felt the force of the wind, he took fright and began to sink. 'Lord! Save me!' he cried. Jesus put out his hand at once and held him. 'Man of little faith,' he said 'why did you doubt?'

Mt 14:25-31

FOR PERSONAL REFLECTION

Reflect on the times you have cried out "Lord! Save me" And you were saved...

have not realised the frailty of their own humanity. And so, the prayer of Peter in the gospel today is perhaps the most heartfelt of all.

It's a prayer that many find themselves using, in one form or another, in these days of recession. It's a prayer that people use when life is at its roughest, during times of illness or despair, times of worry or hardship, times of crisis when we feel trapped and without any choices. But as we know, God doesn't always answer our prayer in the way we would desire. His ways, we are told, are not ours. But we are given the assurance of his love and our value in his eyes. Even if the worst should happen, we will survive; he, our shepherd and guide, will lead us through the valleys of darkness to quiet waters and green pastures. Nothing should cause us to fear, for he is with us. The scripture today tells us to look beyond the storms. It is not in the mighty wind, or in the earthquake or the fire that God revealed himself to Elijah; it was not the wind or the storm that enabled Peter to walk on the water or that saved him when he sank. It is Christ who brings calm and peace; he it is who restores harmony and well-being, so that, when it comes to what really matters in life, we are at peace, untroubled by the storms of life, confident that they will pass, and that we will weather them. For we live in the strength of his presence.

[86] 1 Kings 19:9,11-13
Psalm 144(145):8-9,15-18
Romans 9:1-5
Matthew 14:22-33
[87] Homily given on 7 August 2011

I think that one of the most extraordinary bonds between people has to be the bond between a parent and child. It's really amazing to see how people's lives are transformed by the birth of their children, how they begin to live less for themselves and more for them. It's wonderful too to see the strong protective instincts of parents, as they see to shield their children from the hardships and problems of life, and then how they try to equip them to deal with those difficulties as they grow older. The anxiety of parents for their children's welfare often appears to be greater than that of the children themselves. Parents are often the greatest support that children have in their lives, and that's not just for those in the early years of life, but as we grow older and the relationship with our parents changes, the friendship and support that they offer to their adult children is enormous, from financial help, to help with babysitting and so on.

I imagine many people will understand the anxiety of the woman in the gospel, coming to Jesus, desperately seeking a cure for her daughter. It's easy to appreciate the distress of a mother whose child is suffering and the helplessness she feels in the failure to heal her. And so, this mother comes to Jesus, asking for help. The disciples are eager that Jesus help her, after all, she's tormenting them so much with her pleas. There is only one problem: she is a Canaanite, not a Jew. She does not belong to the chosen people, but to a people who do not share their faith. And Jesus always looks for faith when he heals; his response to prayer is a response to the faith of those who seek him. And so, he reminds the woman that his mission is to the lost sheep of Israel, to his own people. The exchange between them is humorous; in our culture

Jesus left Gennesaret and withdrew to the region of Tyre and Sidon. Then out came a Canaanite woman from that district and started shouting, 'Sir, Son of David, take pity on me. My daughter is tormented by a devil.' But he answered her not a word. And his disciples went and pleaded with him. 'Give her what she wants,' they said 'because she is shouting after us.' He said in reply, 'I was sent only to the lost sheep of the House of Israel.' But the woman had come up and was kneeling at his feet. 'Lord,' she said 'help me.' He replied, 'It is not fair to take the children's food and throw it to the house-dogs.' She retorted, 'Ah yes, sir; but even house-dogs can eat the scraps that fall from their master's table.' Then Jesus answered her, 'Woman, you have great faith. Let your wish be granted.' And from that moment her daughter was well again.

Mt 15:21-28

For personal reflection

During the week, offer a prayer for parents struggling to feed and protect their children.

it might be interpreted as being sharp, but it's actually typical of Middle Eastern humour. "It is not fair to take the children's food and throw it to the house-dogs." "Ah, yes, sir; but even the house-dogs can eat the scraps that fall from their master's table." Here Jesus finds the faith that he is looking for, and he grants the request of the woman.

The story has a number of implications for us. Again, it shows the power of Jesus to heal, and how his care responds to the love of a parent for her child. It also demonstrates the need for faith, that we need to have confidence in the Lord when we pray. But it shows too that the love of God, the message of Jesus is not just for his own people, but for everyone. We are all called into relationship with God; God is the God of all nations; no one is excluded. The love that God has for us is immense, but it is not restricted to any one race or culture or creed. The first reading reminds us that God's house of prayer will be a house of prayer for all the peoples. St Paul tells the Romans that his mission is to them, who are pagans, that the message of the resurrection is for them too. This was a strange message for the Jewish people, who believed that they alone were the chosen people. It can be just as difficult a message for us too, as it brings us into a relationship of love and fraternity with peoples of other nations and faiths; it asks us to look on other peoples as brothers and sisters, equally loved by our God. It challenges any fears or prejudices we might harbour. It calls on us yet again, to welcome those who make their home in this country as our brothers and sisters, equal before God, loved and cherished by him as we are.

The love that God has for us is comparable to the love of a parent for his or her children. It comes from deep within God's being. But all are called into the family of God. His concern for our wellbeing is a concern for the welfare of all. None is excluded. There is nothing partisan, no taking sides. As we gather as one family today at the table of the Lord, may our sharing in this one Eucharist be the sign of the unity we live each day of our lives.

---

[88] Isaiah 56:1,6-7
Psalm 66(67):2-3,5-6,8
Romans 11:13-15,29-32
Matthew 15:21-28
[89] Homily given on 17 August 2008

Who are you? Who are you really? If anyone asked your friends about you, who would they say that you were? Do we ourselves even know who we are? Perhaps they'd answer with our name, perhaps tell our parents' names, what we do, where we live - all things that situate us in the world. But how would we describe ourselves, if anyone asked us who we are.

A few years ago, I was at a talk given by an Afro-American Jesuit priest, a fascinating character. He began by telling us about his grandmother, who said, "Sonny, if anyone ever asks you who you are, tell them you are a child of God." Tell them you are a child of God. Fundamentally that's who we are, children of God, adopted by him and given new life in the waters of baptism. But in our secular society, it's not always how we first see ourselves. If it were, would life be different for us? You are a child of God - this isn't how the world sees us; as Christians, hopefully, this is how we see one another and ourselves. It's a statement made in faith - "I am a child of God."

The followers of Jesus are asked two questions today - firstly who do people say that he is. That's the easy question; they just have to report what they have heard others saying. Then the hard question comes, "who do you say that I am?" That's putting them on the spot, asking them to make their own minds up, to get off the fence, as it were. Peter is the one who answers, "You are the Christ, the Son of the living God." This is not something he could know on his own; this is divine knowledge, given to him by the Father. It's a statement made in faith. Answering in the way that Peter answers involves the commitment of faith; there's no sitting on the fence here - maybe

When Jesus came to the region of Caesarea Philippi he put this question to his disciples, 'Who do people say the Son of Man is?' And they said, 'Some say he is John the Baptist, some Elijah, and others Jeremiah or one of the prophets.' 'But you,' he said 'who do you say I am?' Then Simon Peter spoke up, 'You are the Christ,' he said, 'the Son of the living God.' Jesus replied, 'Simon son of Jonah, you are a happy man! Because it was not flesh and blood that revealed this to you but my Father in heaven. So I now say to you: You are Peter and on this rock I will build my Church. And the gates of the underworld can never hold out against it. I will give you the keys of the kingdom of heaven: whatever you bind on earth shall be considered bound in heaven; whatever you loose on earth shall be considered loosed in heaven.' Then he gave the disciples strict orders not to tell anyone that he was the Christ.

Mt 16:13-20

FOR PERSONAL
REFLECTION

"Who are you?"

you're this, maybe you're that. This is an answer that takes a huge risk.

It is Peter who answers on behalf of the Twelve; he is the one who has discerned the truth of Christ's divine identity, and so Jesus gives him a new name, a new identity. He is no longer Simon, son of Jonah, he is Peter, the Rock on which Christ will build his Church, the First of the Apostles. Since then, Peter and his successors have occupied that central role of leadership among the followers of Jesus, speaking with authority for the other disciples, discerning the truth as it is revealed by God. His new name reveals his purpose, and he holds the power of keys and the assurance of Christ's victory over the underworld. "The gates of the underworld will never hold out against it." With that name comes responsibility, - to be the rock, to be the one who strengthens the others, who holds fast, the one who listens to the voice of God and discerns authentic doctrine.

The next time someone asks you "Who are you," will you answer, "I am a child of God" or would that just be too weird? Why is it weird - to admit the most basic thing that we believe? There's a responsibility that goes with that name 'child of God':

The responsibility to be in reality what we are called by name, truly God's children

The responsibility to be witnesses to God's presence, to his life and his love

The responsibility to love others and to love God

The responsibility to be faithful to the God we served in who we are and in what we do. It's sometimes difficult today to admit to being a person of faith, to tell others that we believe in God, more difficult still to admit that we come to Mass. But if we are God's children, then how can we not respond to his love and gather in his name as his family?

And so we pray to the Spirit for the wisdom to discern who we are as God's children in the world today and the courage to shout it out to the world.

---

[90] Isaiah 22:19-23
    Psalm 137(138):1-3,6,8
    Romans 11:33-36
    Matthew 16:13-20
[91] Homily given on 25 August 2014

Twenty-Second Sunday in Ordinary Time
9293
"Life is hard, lads"

We had a teacher in secondary school, and when, on a night when there was a match on television, we used to plead with him not to give us homework, he'd laugh and say, "Life is hard, lads." I've forgotten the economics that he was trying to teach us, but I learnt the lesson that life is hard, that it isn't always fair, and that a lot of the time, you just have to knuckle down and make the best of it. As young people, we might expect life to be a place where our dreams are fulfilled, where we can become what we want to become, do what we want to do and so on. You might dream of marriage and children or travelling or going to college, getting a job or whatever, and for many these dreams are realised and fulfilled. But not for everyone and not always in the ways we expected, and certainly not without hard work and many challenges. For some, the circumstances of our life and the things that happen have a much greater impact than we could ever foresee, and frequently result in struggles and having to make sacrifices that we did not expect would be required. You might see someone's life curtailed by illness, limited in what they can do; you might find yourself looking after a sick person, or choices limited by our financial situation. Even to be married and to raise a family involves self-sacrifice, compromise and unselfishness.

Jesus talks about the cross in the gospel today; he announces that he himself will suffer, but his followers will also have to renounce themselves and to carry the cross. It's a stark realisation, but in fact, it's no more than what we already know, that life is hard, that it involves compromise, struggle, burdens, suffering, limitations, renouncing

Jesus began to make it clear to his disciples that he was destined to go to Jerusalem and suffer grievously at the hands of the elders and chief priests and scribes, to be put to death and to be raised up on the third day. Then, taking him aside, Peter started to remonstrate with him. 'Heaven preserve you, Lord,' he said 'this must not happen to you.' But he turned and said to Peter, 'Get behind me, Satan! You are an obstacle in my path, because the way you think is not God's way but man's.'

Mt 16:21-23

For personal reflection

How I enjoy and treasure being a follower of Jesus?

121

yourself. What Jesus wants us to do is to keep our goal in mind, to remember that there's something greater, something whose value far exceeds the hardships and trials that life involves. He doesn't want his followers to be discouraged, but to realise that disappointments and hardships are part of life, and to remember where it is that we are going.

You might say that this is a case of 'pie in the sky when you die,' but actually there's something else going on. We don't hesitate to make sacrifices when we believe the goal is worth attaining; think of sportspeople and all the training they do; think of those who work in the emergency services, those who care for the sick; think of yourselves and what you would do for your children, your husband or wife, your parents, siblings, those who are close to you. Ultimately, we look for love; that's the greatest reward or goal of all. We give ourselves out of love; we renounce ourselves out of love; we make sacrifices out of love for another. And God is the source of love, the fulfilment of love. We embrace the hardships of life because our God is a loving God, who calls us to himself, to live in the fullness of love, and our destiny is to be one with him. That is our goal and our destiny and fulfilment, and so many of the challenges that life imposes are teaching us to love and challenging us to do so at a deeper level. As St. Paul says, "I live now, not I, but Christ lives in me." The task of every day is to live in such a way that Christ is living in us, that Christ's love may permeate through us into the lives of others.

The first reading tells us of the reluctance of the prophet Jeremiah to take on the role of God's messenger, as he knew that it would entail rejection, vilification and physical suffering. But stronger than the sufferings he endures is the presence of God, burning like a fire within him, impossible to resist; he was seduced by a greater love, one which drove him to endure torment and imprisonment and all that ensued. We too are loved by the God whose love for us is unimaginable. My prayer today is that as we anticipate our ultimate union with God through our Communion with Christ in the Eucharist, we may also catch the fire of his love and be strengthened to face the challenges that life offers and have the generosity to carry the cross.

The goal of our life is union with God, and that goal should stay before us and encourage us. We are called to live this union even now, just as we anticipate it in our Communion with Christ through the Eucharist.

Christ carried the cross and suffered on it to show us the way. Ordinary life involves the cross; the way of discipleship involves it too, but we are filled with the strength of God's presence, nourished by his Spirit, united with Christ. We think of the Little Way of St. Therese of Lisieux, a way that involved making an offering of every aspect of life, no matter how small. Every joy and every sorrow is offered to Christ out of love, because that love is at the core of our life.

Taking up our cross and following Christ can have many dimensions - from care of loved ones, to accepting the limitations that our responsibilities impose, to having the courage to stand up for what is right and to speak out, risking rejection, to having the generosity and compassion to look out for those in need, to offering the pain we endure in suffering, the hardships experienced when we are in need. St Therese of Lisieux developed the spirituality of the Little Way in order to live in love all the little things of every day. We offer them with love; we accept our lot with patience and even joy; we unite our hurt, our distress, our pain with those of Christ, and we learn to grow in love.

[92] Jeremiah 20:7-9
   Psalm 62(63):2-6,8-9
   Romans 12:1-2
   Matthew 16:21-27
[93] Homily given on 3 September 2017

People who place a high value on the Christian community, the Church, and particularly on coming to church regularly often get frustrated by those who say that they are Christians, followers of Christ, but don't feel the need to be a part of the community, don't come to church. They are more private in their faith and see it as something personal. This tendency is certainly on the increase, as faith and religion become more and more privatised in our society. And yet it is a tendency that is contrary to the spirit of the Gospel, contrary to the actions and wishes of Christ. The phrase he uses at the end of the gospel today sums it up "where two or three are gathered in my name, I shall be there with them." Where two or three are gathered – not one. It's never about one; it's always about a gathering, a community, no matter how small that community may be.

The theme of community continues right through the readings today, and the particular aspect of community that is highlighted is the care and concern we should have for one another, particularly when a member of the community falls into error. The gospel gives the steps that should be taken when a member of the community is in the wrong. Firstly, one individual should strive to correct them. If that fails, then there should be discussion with some witnesses, and the final stage is to bring the person before the entire community. Someone who continues in error is to be regarded as one who does not belong to the community. All the time there is a care and concern for the one who is error, but a care and concern too for the welfare of the entire community. Even when someone is

Jesus said to his disciples: 'If your brother does something wrong, go and have it out with him alone, between your two selves. If he listens to you, you have won back your brother. If he does not listen, take one or two others along with you: the evidence of two or three witnesses is required to sustain any charge. But if he refuses to listen to these, report it to the community; and if he refuses to listen to the community, treat him like a pagan or a tax collector.

Mt 18:15-17

For personal reflection

Consciously pray for your neighbours, friends and family – especially those who have upset you in the past.

regarded as not part of the community, being treated like a pagan or tax-collector, we remember Jesus' own openness to pagans and tax-collectors. He didn't in any way shun them. There is a genuine concern for the person who is in error; their exclusion is about bringing them to their senses, so that they will realise the error of their ways. It's also about protecting the community. The practice described in the gospel was common in the early Church and in other religious communities too.

The prophet Ezekiel uses the image of a watchman, a sentry, to describe the responsibility for the welfare of individuals in the community; he is to watch lest they fall into error, and he is to correct them. This responsibility is shared among the members; the bishops and priests have a particular role here, but it is not theirs alone. Each one of us has a duty of care to our neighbour and that includes the call to correct them. No one particularly wants to do that. If we try, it can be so easy to make matters worse. It should certainly not be done without deep prayer, a sense of peace, and the welfare of the person at heart. It's so easy to allow feelings of anger and self-righteousness take over; our motivation may not always be the wellbeing of our neighbour. But this is always the chief concern of Christ, the one who left the ninety-nine in search of the stray sheep.

Today we are called to love our neighbour. That love is not just about their material needs, but also about their spiritual and moral welfare. We are called to be a community in the best sense of that word, a place where Jesus is present, in our homes and families, wherever two or three are gathered in his name.

---

[94] Ezekiel 33:7-9
Psalm 94(95):1-2,6-9
Romans 13:8-10
Matthew 18:15-20
[95] Homily given on 7 September 2008

TWENTY-FOURTH SUNDAY IN ORDINARY TIME[9697]
FORGIVENESS

People have always found forgiveness difficult. You know the old saying, "to err is human, to forgive divine." It's not something that comes naturally. When we've been hurt or robbed, or lied to, when someone has damaged us in some way, no matter how small, we can find a well of anger rising up inside us. We can find ourselves vulnerable and afraid, or filled with a passion and energy that desires vengeance and retribution. It has always been so. Our first reading from the Old Testament book of Ecclesiasticus shows an awareness of the dangers of resentment, and the potential that it has to lead us into wrong-doing ourselves. The Jews had come up with what in the ancient world would have been considered a very merciful approach to justice in the phrase "an eye for an eye, a tooth for a tooth." Here was a standard that sought to punish the offender by imposing a suffering similar to one that he or she had inflicted. But Jesus sets a new standard of forgiveness for his followers; we must forgive not just seven times, but seventy-seven times, meaning that we are to forgive with a forgiveness that never ceases.

That's not easy. It's not easy to forgive when your heart is hurting, when you've been battered and broken, when someone has diminished you. The standard that Jesus sets is not just something he speaks about or teaches, but something that he put into practice himself. You remember that when he was hanging on the cross, in tremendous physical pain, after a night of imprisonment and torture, here he was being taunted and mocked as he struggled for breath; and yet, he could look at his executioners and the mockers, and say, "Father, forgive them, for they know not what they do." To forgive when the

Peter went up to Jesus and said, 'Lord, how often must I forgive my brother if he wrongs me? As often as seven times?' Jesus answered, 'Not seven, I tell you, but seventy-seven times.

Mt 18:21

FOR PERSONAL REFLECTION

Pray for the gift to Love your enemies.

offender hasn't yet apologised; when they show no sense of sorrow or remorse, when they stand over the offence and will admit no wrong, when they are still hurting, still persecuting us - that's what Jesus did; he forgave his tormenters without any apology or remorse on their part, even as they were inflicting injury upon him. "Love your enemies," - that's what we're called to do, and we know that we cannot do this on our own. Humanly speaking, we are too weak, and we need the grace, the strength, the presence of God to help us. "If we live, we live for the Lord," St Paul says; we need the presence of Christ living in us if we are to forgive. We forgive others not because they're sorry, not because they want to make amends or to start again, although this helps. We forgive because this is who we are - a people called to forgive and to show mercy; a people called to give flesh in our lives to the loving mercy of God, a people called to witness to his compassion and forgiveness, to love our enemies. We forgive for our own sakes, so that we are not burdened by resentment and anger and hatred, and all manner of ugliness that can destroy us and others too. We forgive because we do not want to become angry, hurtful, resentful people. We forgive because forgiveness brings healing and peace.

Forgiveness does not mean that we condone the wrong that has occurred, nor does forgiveness do away with the consequences of the wrongdoing. We might have to protect ourselves so that it doesn't happen again; we might have to take precautions; and the offender must also accept the consequences of their actions, including punishment. But we are the people of God, and we are called to live by a different standard. Sadly, we have failed all too often in our forgiving; too often the Church has failed to forgive, and yet it is key to our mission, key to who we are: God's loving people, called to offer his forgiveness to all.

---

[96] Ecclesiasticus 27:33-28:9
Psalm 102(103):1-4,9-12
Romans 14:7-9
Matthew 18:21-35
[97] Homily given on 17 September 2017

I don't think Jesus would have got on too well if he were negotiating a national pay agreement. Certainly, the unions wouldn't have been too pleased with him, if the story in today's gospel is anything to go by. The employers wouldn't be happy with him either, as the employer in this story paid a full day's wage to those who had only worked one hour. This isn't how business is done. After a week of economic turmoil, it's a bit of a coincidence that we have this gospel story, one which reminds us of the generosity of God to all. However, it also calls on us to be content with what we have and to be generous in our giving. It places a very different set of values before us, and challenges us to think differently about economics, about our attitudes. The values espoused in the gospel story are light years away from the greed and ambition which have characterised much of our recent history. Generosity and care for all are put in their place. At a time when people may well be anxious about their own financial affairs, when money may be scarcer than it has been for a while, when debts may be mounting, Jesus challenges us to embrace the values of the kingdom of God. God loves us with the most incredible and generous love. We can't earn the love of God, because God loves us always with a love that doesn't fail. Those of you with children have only to consider how you love them whether they deserve it or not. You don't earn love.

Always at a time of recession, people tend to re-evaluate their priorities and their lives. If I've spent my life making money, and now find that it's failing me, have I been at the wrong game? Our readings today invite us to consider our goals and

They took it, but grumbled at the landowner. "The men who came last" they said "have done only one hour, and you have treated them the same as us, though we have done a heavy day's work in all the heat." He answered one of them and said, "My friend, I am not being unjust to you; did we not agree on one denarius? Take your earnings and go. I choose to pay the last comer as much as I pay you. Have I no right to do what I like with my own? Why be envious because I am generous?" Thus the last will be first, and the first, last.'

Mt 20:11-16

For personal reflection

Who is Christ for me?
Do I know him?

Do I let him into my life?

priorities. "Seek the Lord while he is still to be found," calls the prophet Isaiah. He calls on us to turn back to God, to remember that the ways of the world are not the ways of God, - and we are the people of God. St. Paul too, writing to the Philippians, is aflame with love of Christ. "Life to me is Christ" he says. That's an extraordinary thing to say; can any of us say it and know it to be true? "Life to me is Christ." Christ is my reason for living; my inspiration, my goal, my driving force. We ourselves are the only ones who know our own true motivation, and sometimes even we are not too sure of it. There are those who appear to have given their lives to Christ, but in truth, they may be just serving their own need for affirmation or pride. But we cannot judge them either; we can only look into ourselves. Who is Christ for me? Do I know him? Do I let him into my life? The values that he taught of forgiveness and generosity – can I really espouse them? Can I follow him even when it is difficult?

A friend of mine said to me once that we're all afraid of following Christ, afraid of really giving our lives to God. We like the idea, but deep down we're afraid that if we follow Christ, we might lose a part of ourselves. Look at the workmen in the vineyard – those who came first had to let go of a notion of fairness that was based on earning to learn one that was based on gift and kindness. We have to do the same – to let go, to trust in the gift of God, who is never ever outdone in generosity. What we lose of ourselves has no real value anyway; what we gain is something far greater. If we want our lives to have lasting value in the world where all investments are liable to failure, then look to the Lord: take the advice of Isaiah "Seek the Lord while he may be found."

---

[98] Isaiah 55:6-9
    Psalm 144(145):2-3,8-9,17-18
    Philippians 1:20-24,27
    Matthew 20:1-16
[99] Homily given on 21 September 2008

Twenty-Sixth Sunday in Ordinary Time¹⁰⁰¹⁰¹
Priesthood

In this Year of Vocation, we are asked today to focus particularly on priesthood. In America, Priesthood Sunday is an annual event, but this is the first time that it has been marked here in Ireland. The invitation to us today is to reflect on the place of priesthood within the Christian community. And priesthood is very much about the community and for the community. It is not about the person of the priest himself; rather it's a call from God to one person to serve the community; it is meant to be a gift for the community. You can judge for yourselves whether it is or not!

Priests are called to follow Christ in his leadership of the Christian community. They imitate his offering of his life to the Father by offering their lives in service. The choice of the priest to be celibate is really about making that offering in a witness that is very real and concrete; it's about saying that the most important relationship in life is our relationship with God. It's also a witness to the kingdom of God. The priest takes the place of Christ in presiding at the sacraments. It is he who says the words that Christ said at the Last Supper "this is my body given up for you." He says these words in Christ's name, but they must also be true in his own life. For the priest also gives his life for those he serves. He is called to witness to Christ's presence at all the significant moments of life – from baptism to illness and death. This is still the great privilege of priesthood – the access to people at the most vulnerable times in their lives, when it is truly an honour to be with them at some significant moment. In many ways priests act as interpreters of life, helping people to understand its meaning in times of life and love and suffering and grief. Traditionally

Jesus said to the chief priests and elders of the people. 'What is your opinion? A man had two sons. He went and said to the first, "My boy, you go and work in the vineyard today." He answered, "I will not go," but afterwards thought better of it and went. The man then went and said the same thing to the second who answered, "Certainly, sir," but did not go. Which of the two did the father's will?' 'The first' they said. Jesus said to them, 'I tell you solemnly, tax collectors and prostitutes are making their way into the kingdom of God before you. For John came to you, a pattern of true righteousness, but you did not believe him, and yet the tax collectors and prostitutes did. Even after seeing that, you refused to think better of it and believe in him.'

Mt 21:28-32

FOR PERSONAL REFLECTION

How do I love the life that God has called me to?

priests have been seen as mediators between God and humanity, representing the people in prayer before God, representing God before the people.

In recent years, the number of priests has diminished, and we have had various scandals and challenges in the Irish Church. They haven't made life easier by any means, but they have brought a new authenticity to the life of the priest. For every Christian, following Christ means taking up your cross every day; for the priest, called to follow Christ in a uniquely dedicated way, these last few years have often been about carrying a cross that is not of our choosing. It has helped clarify what priesthood is about, what being a disciple is about – following Christ even when it is difficult, even when you might want to shirk the burden or run away.

Personally, I love being a priest. I love the life that God has called me to. I love the times of quiet prayer as well as the privilege of presiding at the sacraments. I love the way that priesthood has brought me into contact and into friendship with so many wonderful people. I even love the fact that in diocesan priesthood, we can be moved pretty easily. I feel it gives a great freedom to serve Christ in a spirit of detachment, in spite of all the difficulties that sometimes can ensue. I never imagined the pattern or shape of my life in the years since I was ordained; I never dreamed that I would be in the places that I have been or had the opportunities that I've had. I actually never thought that I'd ever be in Carlow, and I'm here eight years now. And I find that there's something really wonderful in that. I don't know how long I'll be here or where I'll be going next. And that's great. I leave it all to the Lord – I'm sure that I'll be wherever he wants me.

So, I ask you today to say a prayer, if you don't mind, for the priests you know, for the seminarians of our diocese and for those considering a life in ministry. I thank you for your prayers and for your support. It is because of your care and support that we priests can be the people that God has called us to be. Your goodness and your holiness inspire us to be the best priests that we can be and to serve you as you deserve.

---

[100] Ezekiel 18:25-28
  Psalm 24(25):4-9
  Philippians 2:1-11
  Matthew 21:28-32
[101] Homily given on 28 September 2008

The 7th of October is the feast of Our Lady of the Rosary; it's the feast of this church, so it should be a special day for us here in Abbeyleix. The feast day recognises the importance of the Rosary in our lives and in Catholic spirituality. It's a very popular prayer in Irish Catholic tradition, although maybe it has waned a bit in recent years. The diocese published a leaflet last year about how to say the Rosary; it was aimed particularly for use as the Rosary prayed by a family at a funeral.

Why is the Rosary so popular? I think it's because it's very simple and easy to pray, but yet can be extraordinarily profound and lead to a deep union with God and Mary. The simple repetition of the Hail Mary stills our minds, almost like a mantra. Some people pray them very quickly; others take their time. Some may reflect on the words of the Hail Mary, the first part of which comes from the words of the angel Gabriel at the annunciation in St. Luke's gospel; other people do not. As we repeat the words of the prayer, we are invited to reflect on the events of Jesus' life, and so enter more deeply into union with him. The Joyful Mysteries recall the events of his birth and childhood, all of which are recorded in the gospels. The Sorrowful Mysteries invite us to meditate on the events of Christ's suffering and death; again these mysteries are all recounted in the gospels. The Glorious Mysteries reflect on the victory of Christ over sin and death and its effects; the first three, the Resurrection, Ascension and the Coming of the Holy Spirit are all told in the scriptures; the final two, the Assumption of Our Lady into heaven and the Coronation of Our Lady as Queen of Heaven and Earth are very ancient beliefs from

Jesus said to them, 'Have you never read in the scriptures:

It was the stone rejected by the builders that became the keystone. This was the Lord's doing and it is wonderful to see?

'I tell you, then, that the kingdom of God will be taken from you and given to a people who will produce its fruit.'

Mt 21:42-43

For personal reflection

Pay attention to the Rosary this week.

the Christian tradition. Pope John Paul II added five new mysteries, the Mysteries of Light, which recall events from the life and ministry of Jesus. In all of these, we have the opportunity to reflect on biblical teaching and Christian tradition, and to apply them to our lives, and to enter more deeply into union with Christ. We can just say the words or we can really engage profoundly with the Rosary.

Many of you probably pray the Rosary regularly, but if you don't, it really is a prayer worth paying attention to. Its simple format allows us to pray it at any time or place. I often say the Rosary while I'm walking or driving. Its rhythm can be very soothing and calming and is particularly effective at times of death and bereavement, or at times when we find it hard to be still or to focus on anything. The words of the Hail Mary occupy our busy minds and allow us to stop and be still.

October is the month of the Rosary; essentially, it's a family prayer and it might be something that you and your family might consider taking on this month. Some may well pray the Rosary every day, or maybe just a decade, or even once or twice a week. In a parish where our parish church is named in honour of the Rosary, we should really be leading the way in our devotion to the Rosary.

---

[102] Isaiah 5:1-7
  Psalm 79(80):9,12-16,19-20
  Philippians 4:6-9
  Matthew 21:33-43
[103] Homily given on 7 October 2017

"I know how to be poor and I know how to be rich too. I have been through my initiation and now I am ready for anything anywhere: full stomach or empty stomach, poverty or plenty. There is nothing I cannot master with the help of the One who gives me strength." These words come from the second reading, and in the prevailing economic circumstances and the prospect, not to mention fear, of a tough budget, perhaps they are very timely. St. Paul's words point towards a certain indifference to poverty or riches; it really doesn't matter to him whether he's poor or whether he is rich. His confidence is in God; his trust is that the help of God will strengthen him to face whatever it is that life throws at him. All very well, you might say, but he didn't have to feed a family or pay a mortgage or face the pressures of life in the twenty-first century. It's very easy to reflect on what life is about when you have everything you need; when you're struggling to survive, it can seem like a luxury. And yet St. Paul knew what hardship was; he experienced hardship, but it didn't frighten him. The question many people are asking is "how will I cope?" Some may well be asking "can I cope?"

Paul's perspective is one that I think can help us. He is asking us to remember that there's more to life than economics; there's more to life than what we have or have not. In any society, not just one which has been driven by consumerism and market economics, this kind of thinking is very challenging. It asks us to look again at what life is about, about our goals and beliefs and ultimately what we think life is for and where our lives might be going. It's also reminding us to draw on the strength, on the grace that God is offering us each day of our lives, and especially as we come to celebrate the Eucharist. The Word of God offers us a strength and

Jesus began to speak to the chief priests and elders of the people in parables: 'The kingdom of heaven may be compared to a king who gave a feast for his son's wedding. He sent his servants to call those who had been invited, but they would not come. Next he sent some more servants. "Tell those who have been invited" he said "that I have my banquet all prepared, my oxen and fattened cattle have been slaughtered, everything is ready. Come to the wedding." But they were not interested: one went off to his farm, another to his business, and the rest seized his servants, maltreated them and killed them. The king was furious. He despatched his troops, destroyed those murderers and burnt their town.

Mt 22:1-7

FOR PERSONAL REFLECTION

Stop and pray for the brides and grooms you have witnessed celebrating the Sacrament of Marriage.

encouragement which are real and effective. The Bread of Life is food to nourish us for the times we live in as we journey towards the fulfilment of God's kingdom. And it is the kingdom of God which is our goal; we are kingdom people, God's people, invited to the wedding feast. That image of wedding feast is very prevalent in the New Testament; Jesus is seen as the bridegroom, extending a warm and heartfelt invitation to all to join in his wedding banquet. It is not just the Chosen People who are invited but all people, sinners and saints alike. The warnings of the gospel this evening remind us that while the invitation is given freely and generously, it must be properly accepted. We are called to respond with our whole heart.

We frequently hear the first reading from the prophet Isaiah at funeral services. The words act as encouragement to us, pointing towards the day when we will gather at God's holy mountain, and there be fed by him, nourished by him, a time when there will be an end to poverty and hardship, sin and death. This will be a time of abundance. The image is continued but changed somewhat in the gospel, where the banquet is the wedding feast. Both of these images point to the Eucharist; our gathering here and now is already the foretaste of the banquet of God's kingdom. The future promised us has already come. Here Christ offers us the food of the kingdom, his body and blood, to nourish and strengthen us for the life of every day, and all that it may bring. It is the promise that we will share in the final gathering of all. Through our presence and our participation here today, we are saying, "Yes, we want to be part of the kingdom of God; we accept the invitation to the wedding of the Lord." Our acknowledgement of our sinfulness, our celebration of the sacrament of reconciliation, is to recognize that we do not always respond wholeheartedly; our wedding garment, our baptismal garment, may not be as it is meant to be.

Today as we gather at the table of the Lord, we open our eyes to the banquet table that it represents. We ask the Lord to nourish us from this table, so that we may be faithful in difficult times, so that we may not lose heart when the going gets tough. Yes, we can cope; we can and we will. May the Lord of the wedding feast be our strength and encouragement whether we are rich or poor, young or old.

---

[104] Isaiah 25:6-10
    Psalm 22(23)
    Philippians 4:12-14,19-20
    Matthew 22:1-14
[105] Homily given on 12 October 2008

POWER OF NATURE

In the last week, we've experienced the power of nature in a way that rarely occurs in Ireland. Sadly there have been a number of tragic deaths, but for most people it was more a matter of inconvenience than anything else. Some have had the challenge of living without electricity or even water in their homes. The way that nature imposes its presence on our lives from time to time brings home to us just how powerless we are in this world. We're not totally in control; the circumstances of life intrude on our plans, and we have to cope, to sink or swim. We might think we are masters of our own destinies, captain of our ship, but ultimately we're simply pilgrims journeying through a world that is sometimes peaceful, sometimes hazardous, sometimes full of joy, sometimes filled with anguish and suffering.

Our readings today call on us to remember our place in the world; they invite all human authorities to consider their place. The first reading speaks to the pagan emperor of Babylon, Cyrus, who has conquered nations and indeed has acted as God's instrument in different ways, without even knowing that God was there. The word of God is spoken very powerfully to him. Lest he become too proud, God says, "I am the Lord, unrivalled; there is no other God besides me. Though you do not know me, I arm you that men might know from the rising to the setting of the sun, that apart from me, all is nothing." *Though you do not know me...... apart from me, all is nothing.* These are interesting words spoken to the ruler of greatest power of that time over seven hundred years before Christ, and how relevant in a world where many turn their back on God, and

But Jesus was aware of their malice and replied, 'You hypocrites! Why do you set this trap for me? Let me see the money you pay the tax with.' They handed him a denarius, and he said, 'Whose head is this? Whose name?' 'Caesar's' they replied. He then said to them, 'Very well, give back to Caesar what belongs to Caesar – and to God what belongs to God.'
Mt 22:18-21

FOR PERSONAL REFLECTION

Consciously say thanks to others, especially those you have difficulties with!

where leaders and governments choose to forget about God.

An interesting dilemma is placed before Jesus in the gospel, the question of paying tax to the Romans or not. To pay the tax could be seen as collaborating with the foreign, pagan oppressor, disloyalty to the strict tenets of Judaism. On the other hand, the country was governed by the Romans and taxes were due. The answer Jesus gives points to a much bigger picture; give to Caesar what belongs to him; his image is on the coins, so give them to him. But to whom do we owe all that we are, our lives, our world? We are created in the image and likeness of God, so if the coin bearing Caesar's image is to be paid to him, what do we give to God, but ourselves, the gift of our lives? We belong to him.

---

[106] Isaiah 45:1,4-6
  Psalm 95(96):1,3-5,7-10
  1 Thessalonians 1:1-5
  Matthew 22:15-21
[107] Homily given on 22 October 2017

RELATIONSHIPS

Over the last couple of weeks and months, different groups in the parish have been busy preparing the various aspects of the anniversary celebrations for the 175th anniversary of the Cathedral. We've had meetings about the mission, about the various liturgies, meetings about communications, about the parish social, all sorts of meetings. And there have been all the usual tensions that you get as things don't work out and people get frustrated and so forth. All very normal. There was a comment made at one stage; someone said, "you know, it's all about relationships." Anyone who has ever worked on a committee knows the importance of relationships; all of us who are part of families know the importance of relations. It's all about relationships; they are the key to life, the key to living. Our whole celebration of the anniversary of the Cathedral is an opportunity for nurturing relationships, those within the parish and community, at a wider diocesan level, and especially our relationship with God.

It's all about relationships, and essentially that's what Jesus is telling us in the gospel today. "Which is the greatest of the commandments?" His response is to highlight our relationship with God and our relationship with other people. "You must love the Lord your God with all your heart, with all your mind and with all your strength." This is the first and the greatest commandment. As individuals and as community, we are called to holiness. We are called into a closeness with God, a friendship with God, called to know God and to love God. We remember too that the heart of God is relationship; God is a Trinity, three persons, in

When the Pharisees heard that Jesus had silenced the Sadducees they got together and, to disconcert him, one of them put a question, 'Master, which is the greatest commandment of the Law?' Jesus said, 'You must love the Lord your God with all your heart, with all your soul, and with all your mind. This is the greatest and the first commandment. The second resembles it: You must love your neighbour as yourself. On these two commandments hang the whole Law, and the Prophets also.'

Mt 22:34-40

FOR PERSONAL REFLECTION

How have you experienced the love of God in your life this week?

one God. The life of the Christian starts with this journey into the heart of God; that is the first commandment, our first task in life. Even here as we celebrate the Eucharist, we are invited into communion with Jesus Christ; we are called to the table of God, and in the bread of life, God comes to live in our hearts and lives.

This closeness with God is a model for the rest of our relationships. The communion, the union we share with God, is the model for the union and communion we are called to share with one another: You must love your neighbour as yourself. Just as Jesus becomes one with us when we receive him in Holy Communion, just as he lives in us and becomes part of us and we are part of him, so too we are called to be part of one another. Our communion is not just with the Lord; it is with one another. We are part of one another, and the call is love one another as we love our very selves. It's a tall order.

What's interesting about these two commands is the order in which Jesus places them. If you were to ask people to summarise the Christian faith, many would say that it is about following Jesus Christ, who taught us to love our neighbour as ourselves. And so our communities and our churches tend to be good at social projects which help build up the community and serve as acts of love for our neighbour. All very good. But the command to love God comes first. The love of God is the source of our love of neighbour. It is not just because we love God that we love our neighbour; it is also because our experience of the love of God impels us to love our neighbour. The love of God within us is a force calling us into a love, care and compassion for others.

Mother Teresa was once asked why her sisters spent so long in prayer before Jesus in the Blessed Sacrament, would it not be better if they spent more time loving Christ and serving him in the poor. Mother Teresa replied that sisters would not be able to recognise Christ in the poor and serve him, unless they knew him themselves. Let us take the time to know and love God, so that we may also know and love our neighbour.

Have we experienced the love of God? Have we experienced his presence? We have very little spare time in our lives, and even in our Mass, we give very little space to silence and reflection, and yet especially in those quiet moments after Communion when Jesus is present within us, we have an opportunity to stop and listen and to experience his presence. Our love for our neighbour should flow from our love of God. When you see how poorly we Christians have succeeded in loving our neighbour over the centuries, perhaps it is a reflection on how poorly we have loved God.

---

[108] Exodus 22:20-26
   Psalm 17(18):2-4,47,51
   1 Thessalonians 1:5-10
   Matthew 22:34-40
[109] Homily given on 26 October 2008

THIRTY-FIRST SUNDAY IN ORDINARY TIME[110111]
WONDERFUL TIME TO BE A CHRISTIAN

Someone said to me during the week that this is a wonderful time to be a Christian, a wonderful opportunity to be a follower of Christ. That might seem surprising. But this man went on to say that we live at a time when there's nothing material to be gained from our religion; it isn't profitable to be a Catholic. It isn't popular to belong to the Church. Not perhaps since the time of the first persecutions has it been so difficult to belong to the faith community. And because of all of that, those who do believe and who do practise their faith, have to dig that bit deeper. Cradle Catholics, like most of us, can no longer go with the flow, but must delve into our hearts, and allow our relationship with Christ to be at the heart of our Christian living.

The scripture of today's Mass calls for this kind of integrity in our religion. In the first reading, the prophet Malachi castigates the priests who have strayed from the way and have caused others to stumble. That's very contemporary; it could be taken straight from any of our newspapers. In the Gospel Jesus admonishes his disciples to beware of the scribes and Pharisees who parade the external trappings of faith and enjoy the honour it brings them, without really practising what they preach. Society has always put a large store on appearances. Image is hugely important for people today, but there's always the danger of falling into the trap of placing image before substance, and becoming like the Pharisees - all external show, but shallow or even empty inside.

St. Paul puts before us the example of the

Addressing the people and his disciples Jesus said, 'The scribes and the Pharisees occupy the chair of Moses. You must therefore do what they tell you and listen to what they say; but do not be guided by what they do: since they do not practise what they preach. They tie up heavy burdens and lay them on men's shoulders, but will they lift a finger to move them? Not they! Everything they do is done to attract attention, like wearing broader phylacteries and longer tassels, like wanting to take the place of honour at banquets and the front seats in the synagogues, being greeted obsequiously in the market squares and having people call them Rabbi.

Mt 23:1-7

FOR PERSONAL REFLECTION

Allow the crises and challenges of your time to reveal the opportunities and hopes God has for you.

first preachers of the Gospel: "Like a mother feeding and looking after her own children, we felt so devoted and protective towards you, and had come to love you so much, that we were eager to hand over to you not only the Good News but our whole lives as well." Here we have the person who has followed Christ with integrity, not just proclaiming the Good News, but giving his whole life as well. And I suppose that's part of the message of Jesus; that it's not enough to say the words - the Good News, we must truly give our lives as well. Jesus, the Word of God became flesh and lived among us, and that Word must not just remain on our lips but must become flesh in each of us. In our Mass, Jesus nourishes us with his word, the Good News, and feeds us with his own self in the Eucharist, as Paul says, like a mother feeding her children, he gives not only Good News but his whole life as well. The witness we give to him is in ourselves, in the way we live, who we are, not simply in the words we speak; so like Paul, and like Jesus, we also have to give our lives.

And I suppose that's why this is such a good time to be a Christian. The challenges to the Church are an opportunity for us to examine our relationship with God and how we live in the community we call Church - an opportunity that people didn't have in former times. It's as if the crises of our present time are forcing us to really become what we proclaim by our presence here.

---

[110] Isaiah 2:1-5
     Psalm 121(122):1-2,4-5,6-9
     Romans 13:11-14
     Matthew 24:37-44
[111] Homily given on 2 December 2007

THIRTY-SECOND SUNDAY IN ORDINARY TIME[112][113]
COMMITMENT

You hear it said frequently enough that commitment is one of those things that the people of our time find challenging. We find it more difficult to make a commitment or keep one than at any time in the past; it's not necessarily the big commitments, we're just as challenged when it comes to the little ones too. Or so they say. Our gospel today challenges our commitment to our faith. The story of the 10 bridesmaids casts us as the aforementioned bridesmaids, watching for Christ, the bridegroom, to come. That he will come is certain, for he always keeps his commitments. But we don't know when.

The parable concerns a Jewish wedding, where the coming of the bridegroom to take the bride to his father's house was at the centre of the action. The early Christians would immediately have recognised that Christ is the bridegroom, and the Church is the bride, waiting for him to come to take us to the house of God the Father. The bridesmaids keep watch, with lamps lit. The gospel is careful to state that the foolish bridesmaids did bring their lamps; they hadn't forgotten them; they hadn't forgotten to turn up, but they had no oil, nothing stored up. They weren't prepared for a long wait. And as we know, it was a long wait, and it is a long wait. But the gospel questions the half-commitment of the foolish bridesmaids, and our commitment too. Those who follow Christ must be prepared for the long haul. It is to be a long wait, in the darkness, in the night, often with no sign of the bridegroom's presence. But we are to be ready for this. Christians must be fully committed; a half-commitment, like that of the foolish bridesmaids, will not be enough to see us through the darker times of life, the struggles,

But at midnight there was a cry, "The bridegroom is here! Go out and meet him." At this, all those bridesmaids woke up and trimmed their lamps, and the foolish ones said to the sensible ones, "Give us some of your oil: our lamps are going out." But they replied, "There may not be enough for us and for you; you had better go to those who sell it and buy some for yourselves." They had gone off to buy it when the bridegroom arrived. Those who were ready went in with him to the wedding hall and the door was closed. The other bridesmaids arrived later. "Lord, Lord," they said "open the door for us." But he replied, "I tell you solemnly, I do not know you." So stay awake, because you do not know either the day or the hour.'

Mt 23:6-13

FOR PERSONAL REFLECTION

Take a walk and clear your mind of everything except the ground you are walking on and acknowledge the God given gifts all around you.

the wondering and questioning – where is Christ, is he here, is he coming, has he forgotten us? We need to have plenty of oil to keep our lamps burning. The light of faith was given to us at our baptism, symbolised by the light of a candle, lit from the paschal candle. Initially it was entrusted to our parents and godparents to be kept burning brightly. Now we carry it ourselves, hopefully as fully committed followers of Christ.

When times are easy, it is easy to follow Christ. His message of God's kingdom, his revealing of the resurrection and new life and the incredible love of God, these are things that are desirable and meaningful and give us great hope, especially when life is good. But when life is hard, when following Christ means walking the way of the Cross, suffering with him, searching for him, or waiting in the darkness for him to come – this is a different matter, - and there are many whose faith is not enough to see them through. We wonder why. What does it mean to have oil? What is the oil that keeps the light of faith alive, that keeps us faithful in our watching and waiting, that keeps our lamps lit? I think that the oil may have a number of elements. Prayer is probably the main one; prayer is first and foremost about the relationship we have with God. What is your relationship with God like? Could you describe it? Could you describe your prayer life? It's something we need to invest in – and there are different ways of praying, the formal prayers we say, the prayers of offering up the events of every day, the forms of Christian meditation, prayer with the scriptures and readings from the bible, prayer of silence, prayer of contemplation. We need to invest time and energy in our prayer, perhaps we might need to discuss our prayer with someone, one of the priests or sisters, or someone who can guide us; perhaps we need to read about different ways of praying, or become part of a group to find support in prayer. There are many things we can do, but we do need to do something.

Another thing that can nourish us is the scriptures, the word of God. In reading God's word, it can nourish our faith and form the basis for our prayer. Keeping the person and presence of Jesus at the centre is vital. He is the one we look for; look at the story of the bridesmaids; their focus was in watching for the coming of the bridegroom. We too should be focussed on Christ, on his presence and on his coming among us, looking for him when he comes to us in the stranger, in the person in need, in the vulnerable, in the person sitting beside us today. Christ is with us, around us, among us.

Perhaps we also need to be more realistic than the bridesmaids, to realise as a Church and Christian community, that waiting for Christ inevitably entails watching in the dark, struggling, loneliness even, questioning, wondering will he come. Unless we are prepared to face the cross, we are not prepared to follow Christ.

The first reading today calls on us to live with wisdom. The bridesmaids are described as foolish, lacking wisdom, because they are not fully prepared for the watch. Christ is our wisdom. He is the one we watch for; and in all the busyness of life and the challenges it brings to our values and our time, we must not lose sight of what we are about, watching for him, waiting for him, with the light of faith burning strong within us. To live for him is to live wisely.

---

[112] Wisdom 6:12-16
Psalm 62(63):2-8
1 Thessalonians 4:13-18
Matthew 25:1-13
[113] Homily given on 6 November 2011

Thirty-Third Sunday in Ordinary Time[114115]
Talents

Do you know what a talent was? We use the word nowadays to denote our gifts and ability - a talent for music or sport, a talent for art or for working with your hands, a talent for numbers and figures, a talent for relating to people and being able to recognise their needs. There are different kinds of talents and abilities and all of us have been gifted in varying degrees. At the time of Jesus, the word talent meant a large sum of money. A talent was about as much as a labourer would earn in 16 years - so even one talent was an enormous amount, greater than many mortgages. We're told that the man who was going on his journey abroad entrusted his property to his servants - he gave them his life's savings. He took a massive risk, and entrusted them with sums of money that were like the winnings of the National Lottery. And he expected his servants to take risks too, to use what had been given to them according to their ability. What was given was given freely, to be risked, to be used. The first two did exactly that: they took the risk. The third one held back in fear.

The readings today invite us to consider how we serve God, how we use the abilities we've been given.

What is that gift that God gives us that he asks us to risk and to make fruitful? It is the gift of love. Our God has risked everything in giving us the gift of his love, for God is love, and in loving us, he gives us himself. Everything we are, the beauty of the world around us - all are signs of God's love. Love is the one thing that we can give away and in doing so, it grows within us. It's a sure investment. But if we close the door to loving others, if fear stops us

'Now a long time after, the master of those servants came back and went through his accounts with them. The man who had received the five talents came forward bringing five more. "Sir," he said "you entrusted me with five talents; here are five more that I have made."

'His master said to him, "Well done, good and faithful servant; you have shown you can be faithful in small things, I will trust you with greater; come and join in your master's happiness."

Mt 25:19-21

For personal reflection

Reflect deeply on the words of Pope Francis and note the answers:

"Have you thought about the talents that God has given you? Have you thought of how you can put them at the service of others? Do not bury your talents!

146

from taking the risk of reaching out to another in love, we are left alone and in the dark. Fear stops us from doing so many things - fear of being rejected, of being hurt. It is the one big enemy of people. It was fear that prevented the third servant from risking the talent he was given. Love does not grow when it is buried in the ground. Jesus begins the parable by telling us that this is what the kingdom of God is like, a place where all we have and are, are risked for the service of God our King.

A few years ago, Pope Francis was talking about talents and he said the following:

"Have you thought about the talents that God has given you? Have you thought of how you can put them at the service of others? Do not bury your talents! Set your stakes on great ideals, the ideals that enlarge the heart, the ideals of service that make your talents fruitful. Life is not given to us to be jealously guarded for ourselves, but is given to us so that we may give it in turn. ... Do not be afraid to dream of great things!" Pope Francis 24 April 2013

God risks everything in love, and we are asked to do the same.

---

[114] Proverbs 31:10-13,19-20,30-31
    Psalm 127(128):1-5
    1 Thessalonians 5:1-6
    Matthew 25:14-30
[115] Homily given on 19 November 2017

YEAR A

SOLEMNITIES AND FEAST DAYS

St. Brigid's Day[116117]
In honouring Brigid, we honour all Irish women

Standing here before you I feel very honoured to have been asked by the Jubilee Committee to preach at this celebration marking the feast of St. Brigid, national patron of Ireland and patron of Kildare & Leighlin. I want to thank the Committee for their invitation. St. Brigid has always been very significant for me; I grew up not far from the Curragh, which has great associations with her, and my grandmother was reared just yards from her monastery. This woman Brigid has been the inspiration of Irish religious women over the centuries. On the eve of the Jubilee of Consecrated Life, we remember and honour these women, those who spent their lives in the service of God throughout the ages, Irish religious throughout the world, and particularly those here today. In honouring Brigid we honour them. Symbol and story feature strongly in the life of Brigid. The stories may not be true but they help us get to know the woman whose reputation inspired them and fuelled the imaginations of so many generations of Irish people. In telling her story today, we remember the stories of many others too, people of kindness and compassion, of faith and fidelity.

Of the historical saint, we know that she belonged to the Faugharta tribe, a branch of the ruling house of O'Dunlaing, in Leinster. Her birthplace is associated with Faughart in Co. Louth, but also with Umeras, near Monasterevin in Co. Kildare. She was born about 454 and died about 524. Brigid was the daughter of Dubhthach, a pagan and Broicseach, a Christian slave, and more than anyone else she represents the transition from paganism to Christianity in Celtic Ireland. It is fitting that legend records that Brigid was born in a doorway, on a threshold. And in this year of Jubilee it reminds us that, in entering a new

Jesus said to his disciples: 'If you love those who love you, what thanks can you expect? Even sinners love those who love them.
Lk 6:32

FOR PERSONAL REFLECTION

Reflect on the symbols and stories of your life.

millennium, we too have crossed a threshold, and indeed entered through a Holy Door, a symbol of reconciliation for all people and of hope for the future.

In about 480, Brigid founded her monastery at a great oak tree on the hill of Kildare, the church of oak tree. It was a joint monastery, for men and women, but ruled by the abbess. The story goes that Brigid went to a local chief in search of a piece of land on which to build a church, and he told her she could have as much as her cloak would cover. And so Brigid laid her cloak on the ground, and it spread until it covered the area we know today as the Curragh, St. Brigid's Field.

Brigid has always been linked with Mary; in fact, her traditional title is Mary of the Gael, Muire na nGael. She earned that title because, like Mary, she made Christ incarnate, she gave him flesh, in what she said and what she did. She heard the word of God and kept it. She did this through her extraordinary generosity to the poor, and also through her commitment to peace and reconciliation; a lovely story tells how she gave her father's precious sword to a leper to enable him to buy food. In a world where many are hungry and millions of pounds are spent each day on arms, Brigid challenges our society to look again at its priorities.

Brigid is linked with the earth and with agriculture, particularly with ploughing, sowing, milking and butter-making, and she was famous for her extravagant hospitality. One wonderful tale recounts how she turned water into ale, in order to entertain the bishop and other guests on Low Sunday. I am not sure that this was the kind of hospitality St. Paul had in mind, when he asks us in the first reading to make hospitality our special care.

All of these virtues are rooted in and express her love of God, which was the fundamental motivating force in her life. Her spirit of prayer was such that she hung her cloak on a sunbeam. The lavishness of her love for God is expressed in a wonderful poem, from the eleventh century, attributed to Brigid, translated by Brendan Kennelly: In it Brigid says,

I'd like to give a lake of beer to God
I'd love the Heavenly Host to be tippling there for all eternity.
I'd love the men of heaven to live with me, to dance and sing.
If they wanted, I'd put at their disposal vats of suffering.
White cups of love I'd give them with a heart and a half.
Sweet pitchers of mercy I'd offer to every man.

I'd make Heaven a cheerful spot,
Because the happy heart is true.
I'd make the men happy for their own sakes.
I'd like Jesus to be there too.
I'd like the people of heaven to gather from all the parishes around.
I'd give a special welcome to the women, the three Marys of renown.
I'd sit with the men, the women and God,
There by the lake of beer.
We'd be drinking good health forever
and every drop would be a prayer.

- Brendan Kennelly

It seems somewhat ironic to be celebrating the feast of St. Brigid in Rome, in a year of pilgrimage to this city, and in no less a setting than its cathedral church, for by all accounts Brigid was, shall we say, a bit cautious in her attitude to pilgrimage to Rome. Both the Bethu Brigte and the Martyrology of Angus report the story of Bishop Conleth's desire to go to Rome. Conleth was a hermit, a silversmith, whom Brigid chose to be bishop in her foundation at Kildare; evidently she expected him to toe the line. Conleth expressed a desire to travel to Rome, to buy vestments no less; Brigid had apparently given away some others that he had bought there. But Brigid told him not to go, and said to him as he set out "Neither will you reach there nor will you return here." And so it happened that Conleth was eaten by wolves in Co. Wicklow, and didn't arrive in Rome. Beware all would travel here in search of fine vestments!

Brigid, and women like her, were no escapists, but looked for God and proclaimed his presence in the midst of the harsh realities of human existence. Like Patrick Kavanagh, they found that "the light between the ricks of hay and straw \ Was a hole in Heaven's gable." In fact, it is true of Irish women throughout the ages that they lived at the coalface of life, and handed on their faith and love of God to their children, a strong enduring faith that withstood persecution and poverty over the centuries. Indeed, the cross of Brigid was a symbol of the faith that enabled the Irish people to survive in difficult times.

In honouring Brigid, we honour all Irish women. But particularly on this the feast of the most famous of Irish religious and the vigil of the Jubilee celebration of Consecrated Life we honour Irish sisters. Brigid pioneered a unique vision of religious life which nourished the lives of Irish religious through the ages. This was a vision which handed on the Christ-Light, and kept the flame

151

of faith burning. Its great symbol was the fire that burned continually in Kildare from Brigid's time until the Reformation; a flame of faith and of hospitality. These sisters saw Brigid's cloak as a cloak of charity to be spread far and near. Hers was a vision of discipleship based on a close knitted relationship with each other and with God. Here the life of the monastery was such that it gave rise to the word muintearas to express the intimacy of family life. For Irish religious, this intimacy entailed a closeness to the poor, a closeness to the stranger, closeness to the earth. But first and foremost, muintearas was the hallmark of their relationship with God. Listening to the word and keeping it they became sisters, brothers and mothers of Christ. It is no accident that the poet Broccan can call Brigid Mother of the Son of the Great King. Nor is it accidental that she is called Mary of the Gael, Muire na nGael or that the title Mother of Christ was sometimes given to her, for these titles express what we have heard in the Gospel this evening: "Anyone who does the will of God, that person is my brother and my sister and my mother." Following the example of Brigid's discipleship, Irish religious have been mothers of Christ; they have fed his poor, educated his children, healed his sick, visited him in prison. At home and abroad, they have witnessed and continue to witness to the power of God's word and of his love. The model of discipleship they have followed and nurtured called them to look at each person as another Christ, and be sister, brother and mother to them. We give thanks to God for their example and for their presence among us. As the doors of a new millennium open out before us, with the excitement and uncertainty that entails, I pray that Brigid may accompany all Irish religious as they cross the threshold of a new era for religious life.

A Naomh Bríd a Mhuire na nGael, scar orainn do bhrat.
A Naomh Bríd a chroí na féile, stiúir sinn ar an mbóthar ceart.
A Naomh Bríd gheanúil ghrástúil, ar ár namhaid cosain sinn.
A Naomh Bríd a bhean rialta álainn, ar uair ár mbáis glaoigh orainn.

St. Brigid, Mary of the Gael, cover us with your cloak.
St. Brigid, heart of the feast, direct us on the right road.
St. Brigid, gentle, graceful, protect us from our enemies.
St. Brigid, beautiful nun, at the hour of our death call us.

---

[116] Job 31:16-20,24-25,31-32
  Psalm 106(107)
  Luke 6:32-38
[117] Homily given on 1 February 2000 in the Cathedral of St John
  Lateran (Rome)

St. Patrick's Day[118119]
Being Catholic in Ireland today means being conscious of carrying a different cross

Coming to Mass on St. Patrick's Day is an opportunity to give thanks to God for the faith that St Patrick gave his life to preach in this land. Each year it gives us an opportunity to reflect on what that faith means to us at the present moment, what does it mean to be Catholic in Ireland today? At various times in the past few years, and today is no exception, it's been difficult to look at that question. It's hard to be Catholic in Ireland today. It's hard for many people to come to Mass. Many find it difficult to remain in the Church. The scandals of recent years have shattered the faith of some and caused others to lose confidence completely in Church leaders. Many struggle with questions of faith and others struggle with the structures and rules of the Church. The recent discussion about the Tuam Mother and Baby Home has uncovered many questions and it has revealed a depth of hurt and pain, but without really offering any understanding or answers. It's easy to blame, and maybe we should, but there's so much yet to be told that I find it difficult to know where to go in addressing that whole question.

On the other hand, we must still ask - what does it mean to be Catholic in Ireland today? One thing is very obvious to me, and it is that the Ireland of today is calling us to account; at one level it appears to be calling priests and religious to account for the wrongdoing and failures of the past, but I think that a collective societal guilt is also being uncovered and the entire community is being asked to look at ourselves and to keep looking at ourselves. Being a Catholic means that we have to face the past; we have to face the present; we have to acknowledge

The Lord has sent me to bring the good news to the poor, to proclaim liberty to captives.

Lk 4:17

FOR PERSONAL REFLECTION

What does it mean to you to be a believer and a seeker?

the guilt of our community, past and present and come to terms with it. And we remember that we are a community, one Body of Christ, who gave his life for the guilty. We do not lose hope for the sinner.

Being Catholic in Ireland means that we are conscious of carrying a different cross to that of any previous generation. We carry, not pride in the faith of our ancestors which brought them through difficult times, times of persecution, poverty and oppression, but rather we bear the burden of guilt, the awareness of the sins of the past, the failures of our forebears and perhaps also the fear that anyone might look too closely at our own lives. We all share that burden. The story of the darnel in the wheat is particularly appropriate.

I'm not surprised at this, because the faith was preached in this land by a man who was acutely conscious of his own sinfulness, and not just in a general sense. Patrick's mission was questioned and in fact, jeopardised by an old friend, possibly a confessor, who revealed some wrongdoing of Patrick's to those who were to send him on mission to Ireland. We don't know what that sin was, but we do know that Patrick regarded it as a grave sin, which he had left behind him in the past and been reconciled. We nearly didn't have Patrick at all. Our faith was brought to us by a sinner who became a saint. It's not easy to accept that the messenger can be flawed, badly flawed. We saw the Church struggle with that in the case of the late Bishop Eamonn Casey. At least the celebration of his funeral was a recognition of his extraordinary contribution to the Church in Ireland, in Britain and in the Developing World, and not just an acknowledgement of his failures. Our faith was handed on to us by sinners, who may well have become saints. We, sinners, hand on that faith to others, and hopefully we too will become saints, and our sins and those of our forebears will not impede the mission with which we have been entrusted.

Being a Catholic in Ireland today means that we follow Patrick's steps as missionaries. The land in which we live our faith is increasingly hostile to that faith, just as hostile as it was in Patrick's day, or maybe more. We are called to witness to it, to stand up for our faith, to cherish it and proclaim it, as St. Paul says in his letter to Timothy, we insist on it, welcome or unwelcome. That doesn't mean that we're standing on a soapbox all the time; it means rather the witness of our life and practice, our values, our attitudes and our prayer. It means that we can no longer be Catholic in name only but are called instead to a deep and profound awareness of God's presence in us and in our world. We are called to journey into our faith, to deepen our experience of God, to become mystics, as it were. In this too we imitate Patrick, who came to experience a wonderful intimacy with God in the loneliness and fear of days and nights on Slemish as he guarded the sheep. That relationship, the light of God's presence with us, will shine whether we are aware of it or not.

It's not an easy time to be Catholic, but I wonder was it ever, for even in those times when the Church seemed all-pervasive, there were many within and without who were uncomfortable and struggled deeply. Perhaps today it's actually easier to be Catholic because there's no hiding, no pretending, no going along with the flow. Wherever you are with Church today, remember that our focus is always on the Lord we serve, not on his work and not on its leaders, whoever they may be, but first and foremost it is the Lord we serve. My prayer for you on this St. Patrick's Day is that the joy of the Lord may be your strength.

---

[118] Ecclesiasticus 39:6-10
    Psalm 115(116):12-19
    2 Timothy 4:1-8
    Matthew 13:24-32
[119] Homily given on 17 March 2017

LEARNING FROM FAILINGS

Peter and Paul are regarded as the founders of the Church. It was Peter who was named by Jesus; he called him Peter, no longer Simon, Peter the Rock on whom he would build his Church. Paul travelled extensively in the countries of the Mediterranean, starting communities of faith in every city and town he visited, and, with the inspiration of the Spirit, he wrote many letters to these communities, most of which survive as part of the Scripture of the Church. And yet these were real flesh and blood men, with real struggles, character flaws, strengths and weaknesses; their lives were full of ups and downs. Their story is not a story of instant holiness; it's a story of great effort, betrayal, doubt and eventually conversion, commitment and self-giving love. We know Peter the fisherman from Galilee would deny Jesus three times. He comes across in the gospels as passionate and impetuous, captivated by the magnetism of his leader, but at real pains to understand him. At times he is the rock; at other times, Jesus calls him a stumbling block. Paul comes from a very different background. He was a tentmaker by profession, and a highly educated man, having studied with the leading scholar of the day, Gamaliel. He belonged to the Pharisee party, and was zealous in his persecution of the followers of Jesus, until his own conversion on the road to Damascus. Both of these men struggled to find the truth, struggled to do the right thing. They made mistakes and regretted them. But they learned from their failures and turned humbly to God. They became great leaders because of their honesty in searching for the truth, because of their love and because of their utter commitment to Jesus Christ. And they suffered. Paul tells us how often he was whipped and imprisoned; he was even shipwrecked twice. Both of them were executed in Rome about the year 67; Paul was beheaded, and Peter was crucified.

You are Peter, and on this rock I will build my Church. And the gates of the underworld can never hold out against it.

Mt 16:18

FOR PERSONAL
REFLECTION

Reflect on the ways you witness to the love of God.

We could do well to learn from the lives of Peter and Paul. In our own situations, we try to do what is right; we make mistakes; life doesn't turn out as we would like it to. Maybe we don't do as well as we would like at exams. Perhaps we lose our job. Perhaps our marriage doesn't work out. Maybe we lose someone close to us. Maybe we struggle with addictions. But we learn and we continue on; we trust in God who walks with us. Like Peter and Paul, we can be weighed down at times by the realisation of our own frailty, our sinfulness. We can be disappointed when life is harder than we ever imagined. What gave strength to Peter and Paul, what gave them the courage and motivation to keep going, was that they were convinced of the love of the Lord. They knew how deeply Jesus loved them. Peter had followed him from the early days in Galilee; Paul had only his encounter on the road to Damascus after the Resurrection. Yet both of them had this deep sense of Christ's love for them, a love which was greater than anything ever known, a love which was greater than life or death, and which had conquered death to lead to new life. Their courage and perseverance is a great strength for our faith.

Today marks the beginning of the year of St. Paul, a year in which, in different ways, the Church throughout the world will reflect on the life of St. Paul and his message. It's a year in which we are encouraged to read anew the writings of St. Paul and to reflect on them. So much of the New Testament was written by St. Paul – you remember his letters to the Romans, the Colossians, Corinthians, Thessalonians, letters to his companions Titus and Timothy. The missionary journeys of St. Paul testify to his vocation as the apostle to the Gentiles, the one called to proclaim the good news to peoples who had not heard of God. On this feast day, we remember the origins of our faith, how It spread through the work of Peter and Paul and their successors. And we pray that we will be worthy successors of these men, so that we too may witness to the love of God with every fibre of our being.

---

[124] Acts 12:1-11
    Psalm 33(34):2-9
    2 Timothy 4:6-8,17-18
    Matthew 16:13-19
[125] Homily given on 29 June 2008

What is a saint? Someone asked that question recently and it made me stop and think about it. What is a saint? A good person? A very religious person? Someone who is very holy? Someone who does a lot for other people? Often when we think of saints, we have an image of someone who is too good to be true, a very pious person, someone who has suffered a lot without complaining, but maybe we have the notion that a saint is not altogether human. We don't necessarily think of saints as great fun; what kind of craic would you have with one of them? Are saints very solemn and serious? The answer is no, not necessarily; saints are as diverse as the people gathered here. If you were even to think of the saints you know, how different they are. St. Therese of Lisieux, a young girl who chose to enter a convent at the age of 15 and died aged 24; she loved plays and took part in dramas and pageants in her convent. She joined the sisters there in singing and dancing. There are saints like Francis of Assisi, remembered for his embrace of a very radical type of poverty, but remembered too for his love of nature, his ability to see the hand of God present in everything and everyone. There is St. Philip Neri, known as the laughing saint for his joy and good humour. There are saints, who gave up their lives, like St Maximilien Kolbe who died at Auschwitz, offering his life in place of that of a fellow prisoner. St. Anthony of Egypt, who lived as a hermit in the desert and died aged 103. Many of them came from wealthy backgrounds, others, like St. Bernadette, were the poorest of the poor. The saints are as different as we are, with ordinary human frailties.

Traditionally when we say that someone is a saint we have meant firstly that they are in heaven with God, secondly that they could intercede for the needs of the Church and respond to the prayers of people and

This is what he taught them:

'How happy are the poor in spirit; theirs is the kingdom of heaven.

Mt 5:1-2

FOR PERSONAL REFLECTION

Take some time to reflect on the saints you know in your life.

thirdly that they were worthy of being honoured by the Church and having a feast day, perhaps devotions and prayers to them. Today on All Saints' Day, we honour those who have never been recognised or honoured in that last way. There are many saints, who are in heaven with God, who respond to the prayers and needs of Church, but there is no cult or devotion to them. They were ordinary people, who, for the most part, lived ordinary lives. People often pray to loved ones who have died, good people, saints, although perhaps not known by that name. They are models of God's love for us, showing us how to live as Christ did.

In their own lives, they made Christ present through their faithfulness to the gospel. In different circumstances and cultures, facing different challenges and choices, they show us how to follow Christ, how to be faithful to him in the varying circumstances of our lives. They lived with a special closeness to God which we are called to emulate.

All of us are called to be saints too. All of us are called to holiness. Today we ask the saints to help us and to show us how to interpret the gospel message for our time, in our lives, in this century, in this place. Every age and every place has its saints, - the women and men give living witness to Jesus Christ in their faith and love. You and I, we are called to be the saints of this age and this place.

For Catholics, the communion of saints is a very important part of our faith. We believe that the Church is made up, not just of those of us here on earth, those alive at any one time, but that those who have gone before us are still part of the body of Christ. As we celebrate Mass, we believe that they are with us – when we say the words of the Confiteor, we ask Our Lady and all the angels and saints to pray for us. We remember them again during the Eucharistic Prayer. During the Mass, we are close to the saints; they gather with us in worship as we celebrate the one sacrifice, the one memorial of the life, death and resurrection of Jesus which Christians have celebrated for centuries. Many people have a special friendship with their favourite saint, someone they call on in times of need, and those saints are not always the big names – parents, grandparents and other holy people are often the saints we turn to.

---

126 Apocalypse 7:2-4,9-14
  Psalm 23(24):1-6
  1 John 3:1-3
  Matthew 5:1-12a
127 Homily given on 1 November 2008

There's a story told about a bishop in the south of Italy who was dedicating a new basilica – a new shrine. After the ceremony, he was outside and he met a local man called Nico, a poor man who was a bit of a character, and the man asked him, "Bishop, this is a lovely church; but is it a major basilica or a minor basilica?" The bishop turned to him and said, "this is a minor basilica; this is a building which is a house of God; but you, Nico, are a major basilica, because you are a person and you are a house of God."

It might seem a strange thing to be celebrating the feast of the dedication of a church in Rome, but when you think about it a bit, it might not seem so strange at all. The basilica of St. John Lateran is the Cathedral of the diocese of Rome, the church which houses the chair, or cathedra, of the bishop of Rome, the Pope. We might be more familiar with St. Peter's and the Vatican, but before popes ever lived in the Vatican, they were based in the Lateran, and it is still the cathedral church of Rome. Its full name is the Archbasilica of the Most Holy Saviour, St. John the Baptist and St. John the Evangelist at the Lateran. Lateran is the name of the area; the Irish College in Rome is just behind the Lateran Basilica. It is the oldest of the basilicas in Rome, given to the Church by the Emperor Constantine, and it is regarded as the mother church, not just of the diocese of Rome but mother church of all Catholics, the head and mother of all churches throughout the world. So, it's a significant building, one that reminds us of our unity as one church sharing one faith and one baptism.

I have chosen and consecrated this house, says the Lord, for my name to be there forever.

2Chron 7:16

FOR PERSONAL
REFLECTION

Reflect on the awesome-ness of being a living church of God

A church building is symbolic and meaningful, as well as practical and functional. It doesn't just act as a shelter which houses the gatherings of worshippers; it also has a sacred purpose in itself. When a church is dedicated, its walls are anointed with oil as a sign that this building is set aside for a sacred purpose. If you look around the cathedral, you can see the candles and crosses which mark the places where the walls of this church were anointed. A church building reminds us that we are the Church of God; we, the people of God, are his building. We sometimes describe a church as "God's house"; so it is. But so too are we. St. Paul reminds us of that today, that we are the true temple of the Lord. The presence of the tabernacle in the church reminds us of Christ's abiding presence among us; this is a holy place, where God is present in the Blessed Sacrament. But God also dwells in each of us; we too are temples of the Lord. The presence of the Lord in the church building serves to remind us of the presence of God in the church people. And so you find that church buildings in their architecture and decoration reflect the richness of our understanding of the people of God. Here in this church, for instance, we gather in the shape of a cross because the cathedral is cruciform; it reminds us that we are the body of Christ, who died for us on the cross and rose to new life for us. In the Church of St. John Lateran, there are statues of the apostles in the pillars of the Church, giving the sense that the apostles themselves are the pillars of the Church. Our Church is founded on the faith of the apostles and it is the task of the bishops to safeguard and preach that faith. They say that the white walls of the Lateran Basilica remind us that the church is called the bride of Christ, washed clean in baptism and clothed in white to meet her groom in purity and sinlessness.

In the gospel today, we see the anger of Jesus at the misuse of the Temple in Jerusalem, the Holy Place where Jews felt closest to God. But yet the prophecy he makes about raising up the sanctuary is about his own body. He is the true temple, the only real icon of God. Our bodies too are holy places where God dwells; this is why we are called to respect our bodies, and how we use them.

As we celebrate the 175th anniversary of the dedication of the Cathedral here in Carlow this year, we remember that this celebration is about the people first and foremost. This Cathedral represents the unity of our diocesan Church, under our bishop. It is the place from which he presides over the Church of Kildare and Leighlin. It is a symbolic and holy place, and in celebrating the dedication of the Cathedral, we celebrate the faith of the Church, the people of this diocese, and we pray for its renewal and growth. That is why we are having a parish mission as part of our celebration of the anniversary of the Cathedral. You might have seen the monks who will lead the mission on Would you Believe last Sunday night.

As we honour our holy places, we pray that we may honour our church and ourselves as the dwelling place of God's spirit.

---

[128] Ezekiel 47:1-2,8-9,12
    Psalm 45(46):2-3,5-6,8-9
    I Corinthians 3:9-11,16-17
    John 2:13-22
[129] Homily given on 9 November 2008

THE CHRISTIAN STORY IS A STORY
OF REDEMPTION AND RESTORATION

I've always been fascinated by the story of Adam and Eve. Although it was one of the last books of the Old Testament to be written, it's the very first thing that we read in the bible at the start of the book of Genesis. It's a foundation story, one that tries to explain the condition that the human race finds itself in, with all the problems, tragedies, and unhappiness that people face. Since the first people walked the earth, sin has been part of the human story; we cannot avoid it. But the story of Adam and Eve also affirms God's love for his people and his pride in them. Although they have been flawed by evil, people are basically good as they are formed in God's image.

Right from the beginning, human beings are created to live in the presence of God. They are at ease in God's presence and see God face to face. They are also very much at ease with themselves, and experience a unity and a harmony between body, spirit and soul. But all of that changes. The piece that we have read in our first reading today focuses on the sin of Adam and Eve and their discovery by God. Because they have sinned and disobeyed God, something has happened to Adam and Eve. They are no longer at ease in the presence of God, nor are they at ease with themselves; they are uncomfortable in their own skin; the harmony has been broken, and so they hide. They cover themselves. They hide from God, but they also hide from themselves. Here we have the root of the alienation that is part of the human experience: alienation from self, from God, from one another.

The Christian story continues the story that began with this first couple; it is a story of redemption

'It is noy those who say to me, "Lord, Lord," who will enter the kingdom of heaven, but the person who does the will of the Father in heaven.'

Mt 7:21

FOR PERSONAL
REFLECTION

"Hail Mary, full of grace... Our Mother, our model and our inspiration.

and restoration. God sends a new Adam to the earth, a new man, Jesus, who will lead the world and its peoples through the darkness of the sin and suffering and death that are the result of the first sin and bring them into a new relationship of life with God. His coming marks the start of a new creation. Jesus is the sinless human being, born of Mary, who is the new Eve. The first Eve, the mother of humanity, was a sinner and the mother of sinners; the second Eve, Mary, has been kept free from sin, so that her children would be a sinless people. And that's the part of the story that we celebrate today – Mary was preserved from any stain of the Original Sin from the very first moment of her existence. She was immaculately conceived. This belief in the Immaculate Conception has been held by Christians since the earliest days of the Church, but it wasn't defined as a dogma of our faith until 1854, when Pope Pius IX defined it. It was only four years later that Our Lady appeared to a young girl, Bernadette Soubirous in the French village of Lourdes, and identified herself as the "Immaculate Conception."

The dogma of the Immaculate Conception has always been controversial; but there is a very strong and ancient tradition of faith for it. When we pray the "Hail Mary", we say "Hail Mary, full of grace." These words are a version of the angel Gabriel's greeting to Mary in the gospel today. We all of us receive God's grace in our lives, but Mary received God's grace without any obstacle; she is the only one of whom it can be said that she is "full of grace," and this because, from the moment of her conception, right from the beginning of her existence, there was no impediment to grace in her. She is highly favoured indeed.

The feast of the Immaculate Conception is an important step in the celebration of Advent and Christmas. It prepares for the coming of the Saviour by placing Mary before us as the first sign of the fulfilment of God's promise that he would redeem his people. Since sin caused people to hide from God and from themselves, God sent his Son to his people, to bring them back, to reconcile them with God, with one another and with themselves – to end the alienation that disfigures humanity. Our salvation is coming; the Messiah is at hand. Our destiny is to live through love in God's presence as God's children in Christ; its fulfilment has already begun.

---

[130] Isaiah 26:1-6
    Psalm 117(118):1,8-9,19-21,25-27
    Matthew 7:21,24-27
[131] Homily given on 8 December 2016

The Funeral of Con Cummins Snr.[132]

I think that the one memory I have of my father which overrides all others is the memory of him standing at the door. He spent a lot of time standing at our front door or the door of the bar. When we were small children and Auntie Judy worked in Dublin, he would bring us to the door with him to wait for her to come home on the bus. All my life Daddy stood at the door waiting to welcome whoever it was home. Many's the time we arrived from wherever we were, and there he'd be, waiting. It was a place that suited him, a place to meet people, to hear the news. You wouldn't know who he'd meet on the street and bring in; my mother got some rare surprises, and she'd say "Who's he going to bring in next?" When his children were born, he would bring us out onto the street to see who he'd meet to show off the new baby. He did it even when Con was born in the snow. And true to form, he sneaked off one day with his grand-daughter, Caoimhe, brought her to the door to see who he'd meet to show off the new child. And that picture of Dad at the door is one that many people have of him; so frequently people have said to me, I met your father at the door, and he said this that or the other. He was a real extrovert and loved people and being with people.

For us his family, I think the image of Dad at the door is much more than just a memory. It really said so much about who he was. Always welcoming, wanting his family to be at home with him. Ready to welcome us no matter what. And not just us. I always associate him with the loving father in the story of the Prodigal Son, - of course not admitting for an instance that he had any prodigal children!! But the love of that prodigal father that seemed to journey with his son and brought him home for me describes so perfectly what I and my sister and brothers experienced in our relationship with Daddy. At times I used to wonder at his generosity and the love that was in his heart; I certainly couldn't match it. And I wonder how God could be more loving than Dad was. And yet God will not be outdone in generosity. I often hear that children receive their image of God from their parents; and from Dad, we learned to know God as a Father who is boundless in love and mercy and forgiveness, not so much from what Daddy said, but from who he was and how he behaved. He gave flesh to the love of God; he made it incarnate. And that loving Father in heaven was waiting

---

[132] Homily given on 24 February 2003

at the door his house with many rooms on Saturday to welcome Daddy home just as he welcomed so many. And you can be sure that if there are many rooms in God's house, then Dad will have a radio in every one of them.

Growing we heard many stories about Dad in the pantomime and in plays and on the stage. It was like living with a myth, or with someone who had a hidden life, because none of his children ever saw Dad perform on stage, only to sing the occasional song. And sometimes we found it difficult to believe in that part of his life, a part that people still talk about so many years after he gave it up. But to say that we never saw him on stage doesn't mean we never saw him acting - because he was constantly performing, and you never knew when to take him seriously or not. He was very proud of the Pantomime Troup in Newbridge, particularly because it was a parish group. He loved the parish; he loved Newbridge and was always very proud of his roots here and taught us to take pride in it too. He loved County Kildare and took great pride in telling people that the most important Irish people were all from Kildare - from St. Brigid, Ireland's patron, to St. Laurence O'Toole, Ireland's first canonised saint, to the greatest Irishman that ever lived, Arthur Guinness.

For a publican, he had an unusual relationship with his business. He loved his customers; they were family to him. And yet he was very aware of alcohol abuse and the dangers associated with it and preached the evils of drink to anyone who'd listen. The bar was Dad's life. He loved the atmosphere, the people. The bar was his work and his hobby. And he found it difficult not to be in the thick of the action when his health was worsening. He was an old-fashioned publican in many ways, with high standards for himself and for others, and yet great patience with those who didn't meet them.

Our first reading spoke of a time for all things. For the Cummins family, these last weeks have been a time for dying. The deaths of Dad's brothers, Tom and Joe, at Christmastime grieved him deeply. They were very close. These deaths, coming so soon after the loss of his brother-in-law, Paddy Harkin last March, who was a great friend of Daddy's, these deaths were very hard on him. And so there is a time for grieving and for mourning. But if there is a time to die, there is also a time to be born and Daddy was really looking forward to the birth of his second grandchild, due next month. Dad was a very proud grandfather.

It is perhaps my mother who will miss him most. Dad paid tribute to her during the week, and he was telling of how he had prayed that he would find the right wife, and he said, look, it was perfect. You only had to notice how he looked at her and she at him to be aware of the depth of their love and union.

My mother has lost her best pal. Conleth, Garrett, Maria and I have lost the dearest of Dads. And yet today we thank God for the privilege that was given to us of having Con Cummins as husband and father. Our hearts are filled with grief and gratitude, and we entrust him to the God of Welcomes and hospitality. May he rest in peace.

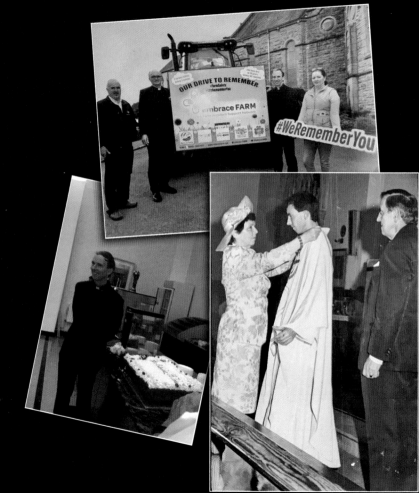

Fr John Cummins RIP
17 October 1966 - 30 January 2019

Jesus Wept![132]

"Jesus wept" (John 11:35), reputed to be the shortest sentence in the Bible but certainly one that gives a lot more to all of us that just two words.

In chapter 11 of John's Gospel, we hear how Jesus wept when he arrives in Bethany to be told that his friend Lazarus is dead and already in his tomb. His reaction revealed his humanity and the vulnerability of those who grieve. All this happened as Jesus was making his way to Jerusalem to celebrate his last Passover with his disciples.

Often there is an expectation that believers should be able to handle grief and pain without showing their emotion, as if showing emotion is a sign of weakness or a sign of a lack of faith. This expectation is stronger for priests and religious. Expectations are only our limited expectations, and they are usually moulded by our upbringing!

On 30 January 2019, many of us received phone-calls to let us know that a good friend, John, had died suddenly. He was a parish priest in a busy town, and he lived his priesthood every minute of the day. He had just come in from visiting the local primary school and somehow his car went out of control on the hill outside his house and he died. The shock resounded through the area and the ripple effect could be felt across the country as classmates gathered to pay their respects and to pray for his family and friends.

From the Wednesday evening of his death to his burial on the following Monday, the days played out in slow motion and one couldn't help but see the similarities between the funeral journey and the Easter journey we celebrate each year. We can often attend an Easter Triduum without any feeling for the events that are being replayed. We just go through the motions and maybe offer a comment or two on the quality

---

[132] Pender, P (2019 May/June) Jesus Wept! Spirituality (Dominican Publications) Volume 25 131-133.

of the liturgy or the length of the sermon! But the funeral of a friend is so different and this I believe is what Jesus found when he arrived in Bethany.

When I arrived in town on Friday evening to pay my respects, I was struck by the stillness and a raw sense of sadness. The long queue in the church shuffled quietly up the aisle. Every now and then, I could hear sniffling and a gulp from someone who was unsuccessful in holding back their tears and upset. A group from the parish had refreshments for the mourners and a space for us to meet and exchange memories and offer each other support. At the end of the evening we adjourned to the church for Night Prayer before returning home to prepare for the first of two Requiem Masses.

The following day we reconvened in the church for the first Requiem Mass. Sitting a few rows behind the family, I watched as they ministered to each other. A gentle arm around a mother mourning her son and an embrace for a brother and sister. As the clergy processed into the church, they looked sad, vulnerable but at one in their grief. They were fraternal in their support for each other. The words spoken by John's bishop were a compendium of the words given to him by many who had known John. The bishop was inundated with texts and emails once the news of the untimely death was made public and his words on this occasion were drawn from these texts and emails, as well as his own experiences of John.

After Mass, people huddled together and as the hearse pulled away from the church there was an impromptu round of applause from the parishioners who had formed a guard of honour along the avenue. As the cortege made its way out of town, the crowd grew in numbers then stopped at the top of the town to pray and say the last goodbye before the hearse continued on its journey to John's hometown.

I left the town that afternoon with the feeling that I had been ministered to by everyone I met. Surprisingly there were no pious platitudes. Everyone spoke honestly about how they were feeling, and their honesty was refreshing, shocking and wonderful. John's death was all too soon and came at a time when the church in Ireland needs more and more men like him. On Sunday, many of us spent the day back in our own parishes while the people of John's hometown had time to pay respects to John and his family.

The second Requiem Mass took place on Monday with an equally passionate send-off from everyone. The words delivered by his close friend and classmate resounded with everyone who knew him. Smiles and tears in equal measure! I felt tears flow down my face so many times during the ceremonies, I gave up trying to hide my upset. John's family and friends instinctively gave permission to everyone to express their feelings. It was a great gift to all of us and a witness to their strength and belief in the Gospel. It was also a testimony of their gift of John to the priesthood and an endorsement of his calling. The final words were delivered by John's older brother and were taken from one of John's sermons.

"We turn to our God, as people have done for centuries and ask why? Why this pain, this loss, this tragedy? The only answer God gives is the gift of his Son… And God's Son came not to take any of that pain away, not to give us any easy answers. He came to be with us, to live as we live, and to die as we die; and in his dying, to promise a life without end in the resurrection, – to lead us and show us the way. That is our faith; that is at the heart of being a Christian – our belief in the resurrection. We believe that our God is with us at every moment of life, no matter how difficult that moment may be. Even in our grief he is with us, even now. Death separates us from those we love, but only for a time. It seems so final, but they are not lost to us because they are with God and God is very near. In the gospel, Christ invites us to come to him, to put our trust in him that he will lead us through these days and be a light to guide us in this dark time. The burden of grief is one of the heaviest to carry … but Christ asks us to come to him, to find our strength in his love and in his presence with us"

Words from the deceased delivered with passion are hard to follow but we must leave the church and move on even though staying is a more attractive prospect. Sounds strange! What we would have given to suspend time and stay together. Suspending time not being an option, we had to let go of John formally and start living in our changed state.

Over twenty-seven years ago, the bishop at John's ordination to Priesthood, reminded John that he and all priests are "in persona Christi" – in the person of Christ. As the procession of priests processed out of the church ahead of his coffin, every priest was weeping and some crying openly. Strength to be like Jesus – strength to weep as Jesus did when he too lost his friend. This was probably the most powerful priestly witness I have seen for many years. We are all vulnerable beings doing our best in situations that we never imagined we would be in; doing our best to live up to our calling.

ACKNOWLEDGEMENTS & THANKS

The Cummins family would like to acknowledge and thank the following, without who, producing this book would not have been possible:

- Bishop Denis Nulty
- Bishop Ger Nash
- David Connaughton
- Neasa & Dominic Reigh
- Paddy Pender
- Fr Ger Ahern
- Joe O'Brien
- Julie Kavanagh
- Maeve Mahon
- Mochua Print
- Sharon Butler

- Siobhan McNulty
- Christine Ogoldsby
- Dawn & Aidan Cunnane
- Neasa Hogan
- Caoimhe Cummins
- Fr Liam Morgan
- Fr Paddy Byrne
- Fr Tom O'Byrne
- Fr Ruairí O'Domhnaill
- Fr John Harris O.P.

Photographs courtesy of:

- The Cummins family
- Bishop Denis Nulty
- Leinster Express

- Bishop Ger Nash
- Carlow Cathedral Parish Office
- Embrace farm

Photo Index: